ARMS AND UNIFORMS · 1

ARMS AND UNIFORMS

Ancient Egypt to the 18th Century
18th Century to the Present Day

The Napoleonic Wars Part 1
The Napoleonic Wars Part 2

LILIANE & FRED FUNCKEN

Arms and Uniforms · 1

Ancient Egypt to the 18th Century

WARD LOCK LIMITED · LONDON

© Illustrations Casterman 1967
© Text Ward Lock 1972
Reprinted 1974
ISBN 0 7063 1814 5

First published in Great Britain in 1972
by Ward Lock Limited, 116 Baker Street,
London, W1M 2BB

All Rights Reserved. No part of this publication may be reproduced, stored in a retrieval system, or transmitted, in any form or by any means, electronic, mechanical, photocopying, recording, or otherwise, without the prior permission of the Copyright owner(s).

Contents

1	Egypt	10
2	Assyria	16
3	The Medes and the Persians	24
4	Greece	30
5	The Etruscans	52
6	Rome	54
7	Gladiators	70
8	The Gauls	72
9	The Great Invasions	80
10	The Huns	82
11	The Franks	84
12	Anglo-Saxons and Carolingians	86
13	Vikings and Saracens	90
14	The Feudal Armies	92
15	The Armies of the 12th Century	96
16	The Armies of the 13th Century	102
17	The Hundred Years' War	108
18	Artillery and Firearms	112
19	The Armies of the Renaissance	116
20	Reiters and Lansquenets	120
21	Mercenaries and Horsemen of the 16th Century	122
22	The Armies of the 17th Century	124
23	The Armies of the First Half of the 18th Century	142
24	Index	151
		155

1 Egypt

For more than 4,000 years the Egyptian pharaohs fought, with varying success, many invaders seeking to occupy their rich lands. Sometimes they marched up the Nile to contain the Negro tribes, or they fought Asiatics infiltrating through the Isthmus of Suez – people who themselves were under pressure from the conquering hordes of Assyrians and Hittites.

Most of the pharaohs confined their activities to defending frontiers or sudden raids, but Thotmosis (1540–1505 BC) and Rameses II (1292–1225 BC) and III (1198–1167 BC) embarked on a series of campaigns that extended their empire as far as the Euphrates.

In battle the pharaoh – the incarnation of Horus, child of the Sun-God and King of the Universe – wore body-armour of various colours and a broad enamelled collar held by a golden chain. On his head he wore the *kopersh*, a war-helmet carrying the design of a serpent. He rode in a richly decorated chariot drawn by two horses crested and protected by thick padded blankets. Horses were brought into Egypt by the Hyksos invaders. Round the person of the pharaoh there would be a host of light chariots each ridden by two warriors.

The army was made up of professional soldiers, sons often following their fathers in the service. In exchange for their services the pharaoh would grant them portions of land which could be confiscated if they ever refused to obey the call to arms.

Behind them came the mass of the heavy infantry. They were bare-chested, the lower body protected by a loin-cloth strengthened

1, Egyptian pharaoh in his chariot. In his right hand he holds a whip and sickle. 2, ordinary type of chariot.

1

2

with patches of leather.[1] Instead of helmets, on their heads they wore heavy wigs of horsehair, wool or palm-fibre. They carried copper-tipped spears[2] and a wooden shield painted or covered with leather.

The light infantry was formed of archers armed with bone or flint-tipped arrows with which they harassed the enemy before the main attack. The bow they used, with its curious break in the middle, has never ceased to puzzle archaeologists. No remnant of this weapon has ever been found, only frescoes and murals show us what it looked like, and even then in insufficient detail. It is generally agreed that the bow was made in two pieces joined together at an obtuse angle. But how? Perhaps it was done by a strong horn joint that acted as a spring.[3]

Certain units of picked men wore protective clothing made up of several thicknesses (sometimes eighteen) of material stuck together after being soaked for a long time in salted wine. It may not have offered much protection against pointed weapons, but it was very effective against blunt instruments.

The mercenaries were numerous and highly valued. There were natives from the Sudan, Lydians and the warlike Shardans from Tripolitania, renowned for their bravery. Later their numbers were increased by Greeks.

A large number of recruits were raised from among the peasants, but they were more decorative than useful. The Egyptian loved life too much – and who can blame him? – to make a good soldier. These men marched under the burning sun, their dragging feet

1, Egyptian foot-soldier. 2, archer of the light infantry. 3, pharaoh in battle order. 4, Numidian archer. (Numidia corresponds geographically with the Algiers of today) 5, Numidian standard-bearer. 6, officer, 'Corps d'Elite', in protective jacket. 7, soldier with the standard used for transmitting orders. 8, soldier with crocodile-skin jacket. 9, soldier armed with sickle and single stick.
10, Sudanese auxiliary. 11, 12, 13, 14, arrowheads. 15, spear-heads. 16, 17, bows. 18, 19, 20, Neolithic flint weapons. 21, dagger. 22, spear-head. 23, bladed mace. 24, dagger. 25, 26, ceremonial axes. 27, sickle. 28, 29, 30, daggers.

---

[1] p. 13, *9*; p. 15, *8*. [2] p. 13, *1/15/22*. [3] p. 11, *1*; p. 13, *10*.

13

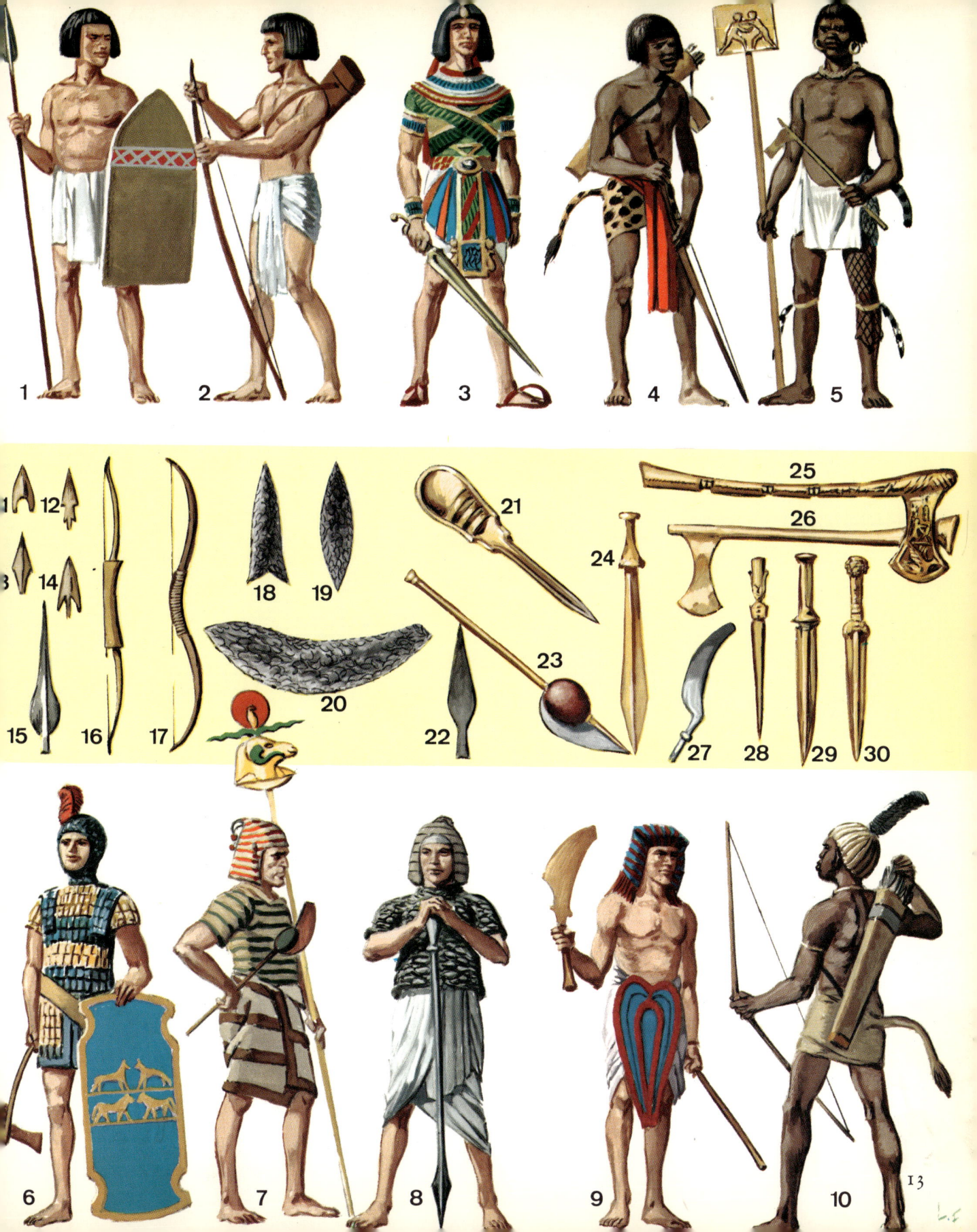

throwing up clouds of dust that, seen from far off, struck fear into the enemy. The conscripts were poorly armed with pikes, javelins and slings; their shields were two lengths of wood joined together and crudely painted in imitation of cowhide.

The officers were equipped very differently. They wore coats of mail, tunics reinforced with metal scales[1] or sometimes made of crocodile skin. Their helmets were of leather or some thickly padded material. They had various weapons – swords, short swords, single sticks, daggers and axes.

In action the movements of the different parts of the army were controlled by signals given with special standards mounted on long poles.[2] A system of 'decorations' was evolved: collars of gold or silver, and weapons of honour.[3]

The Egyptian did not change over thousands of years – except perhaps that his distaste for the military virtues grew steadily stronger. Eventually he left the business of defending his country entirely in the hands of mercenaries. An old man described to his son the lot of the soldier: "He carries his food and water on his shoulders, like a donkey with a broken back. He drinks foul water. He trembles like a little bird in the face of the enemy. When he returns to Egypt he is nothing but a worm-eaten old faggot"

1, Egyptian pharaoh's foreign bodyguard. 2, Semite auxiliary. 3, Spiked helmet. 4, Hittite helmet. 5, Philistine foot-soldier. 6, Philistine chariot. 7, Egyptian chief's shield. 8, Egyptian soldier and shield with hole. 9, mace with hand-guard. 10, short-sword. 11, arrow quiver. 12, military emblem. 13, spear-breaker. 14, short-sword. 15, Temehu auxiliary.

1 p. 13, *6*.   2 p. 13, *7*; p. 15, *12*.   3 p. 13, *25–26*.

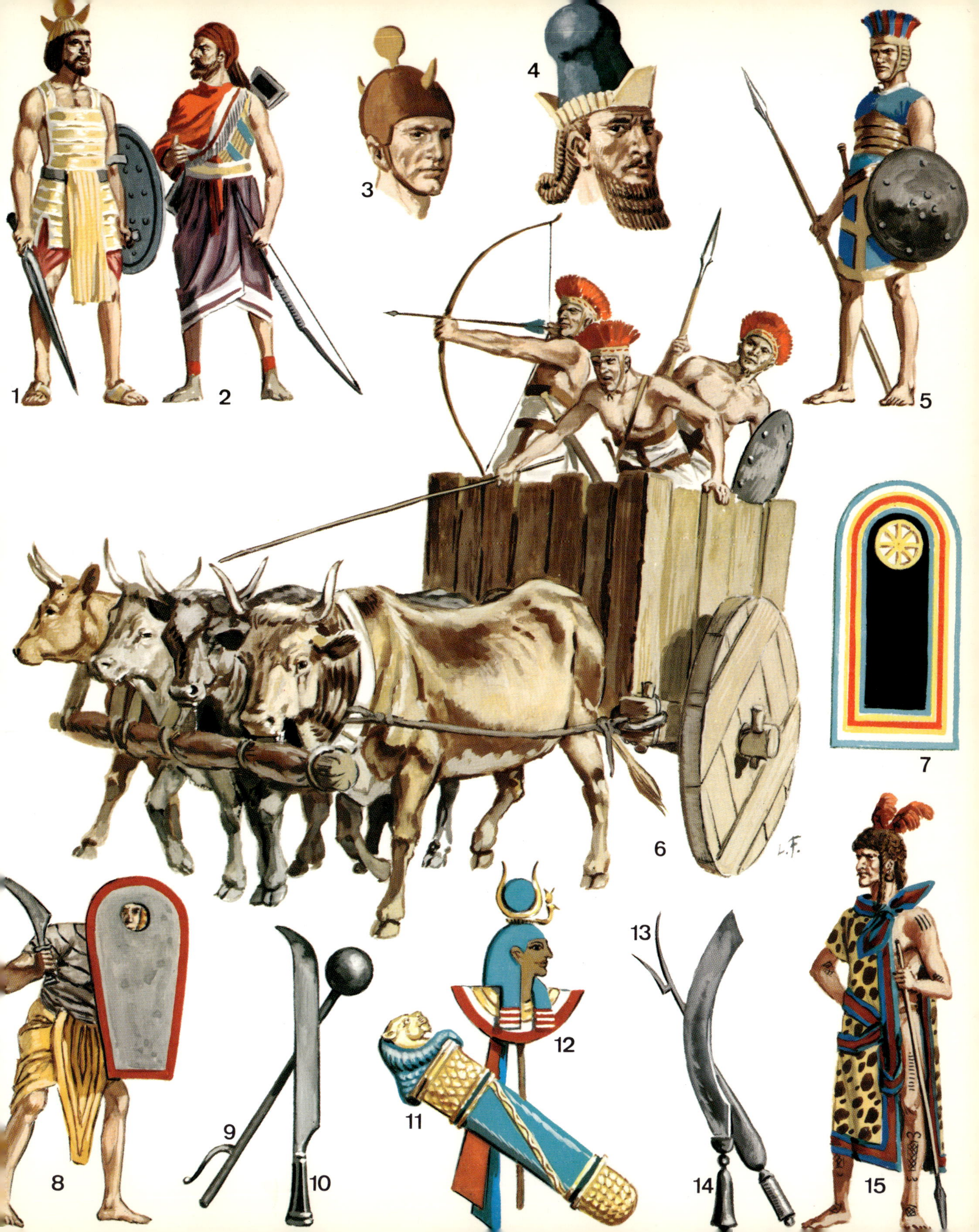
1
2
3
4
5
6
7
8
9
10
11
12
13
14
15
L.F.

Assyria

During the 18th Dynasty the little kingdoms of the Euphrates were under the rule of the great conquering pharaohs – but contact with the invaders gradually developed an aggressive, warlike instinct in the Chaldeans.

By 1125 BC the Assyrians had grown powerful and were making their first conquests in Armenia, Syria and the Chaldeans under the leadership of Tiglathpileser I. Victory succeeded victory. Ashurnasirpal invaded Syria, Mesopotamia and Judea. After him Sargon made more conquests. The enraged Egyptians threw their allies, Syria and Israel, against Assyria. Sargon routed them, forcing the Egyptians to intervene. The battle took place at Raphia, to the south of Gaza, in 720 BC, and once again Sargon was victorious; as a result he opened up the way for his successors Sennacherib, Esarhaddon and Assurbanipal, who invaded the Egyptian Empire, seized Thebes in 662 BC, and went on to occupy the whole of Egypt.

Who were these warriors against whom no one could hold out? They were undoubtedly the finest army in the world – unified, trained in all military tactics, cunning in ambush and methodical in sieges. No one could stop them, whatever the nature of the terrain. In the field, the Assyrian army could muster a whole range of specialist units.

We can imagine the spectacle of this army marching out of the sumptuous gate of Ishtar, with its decorations of glazed bulls and griffins, as the spirals of smoke from a sacrifice rose above the summit of the Tower of Babel.

Crowds of people would be cheering the soldiers from the rooftops and packed together on the walls of fired bricks cemented with tar. These formidable walls were 50 m/164 ft high and 25 m/82 ft across (wide enough to allow two four-horse chariots to pass one another). They were protected by 250 square towers and pierced by 200 bronze gates.

1, 2, 3, 4, 5, types of Assyrian helmet. 6, quiver in moulded leather. 7, bow and arrow. 8, dagger with hilt in form of horse's head. 9, wooden shield. 10, shield in enamelled bronze. 11, 12, 13, axe-heads. 14, Assyrian emperor in his chariot. 15, 16, swords. 17, double-bladed axe. 18, sickle-head. 19, mace. 20, sword. 21, axe-head.

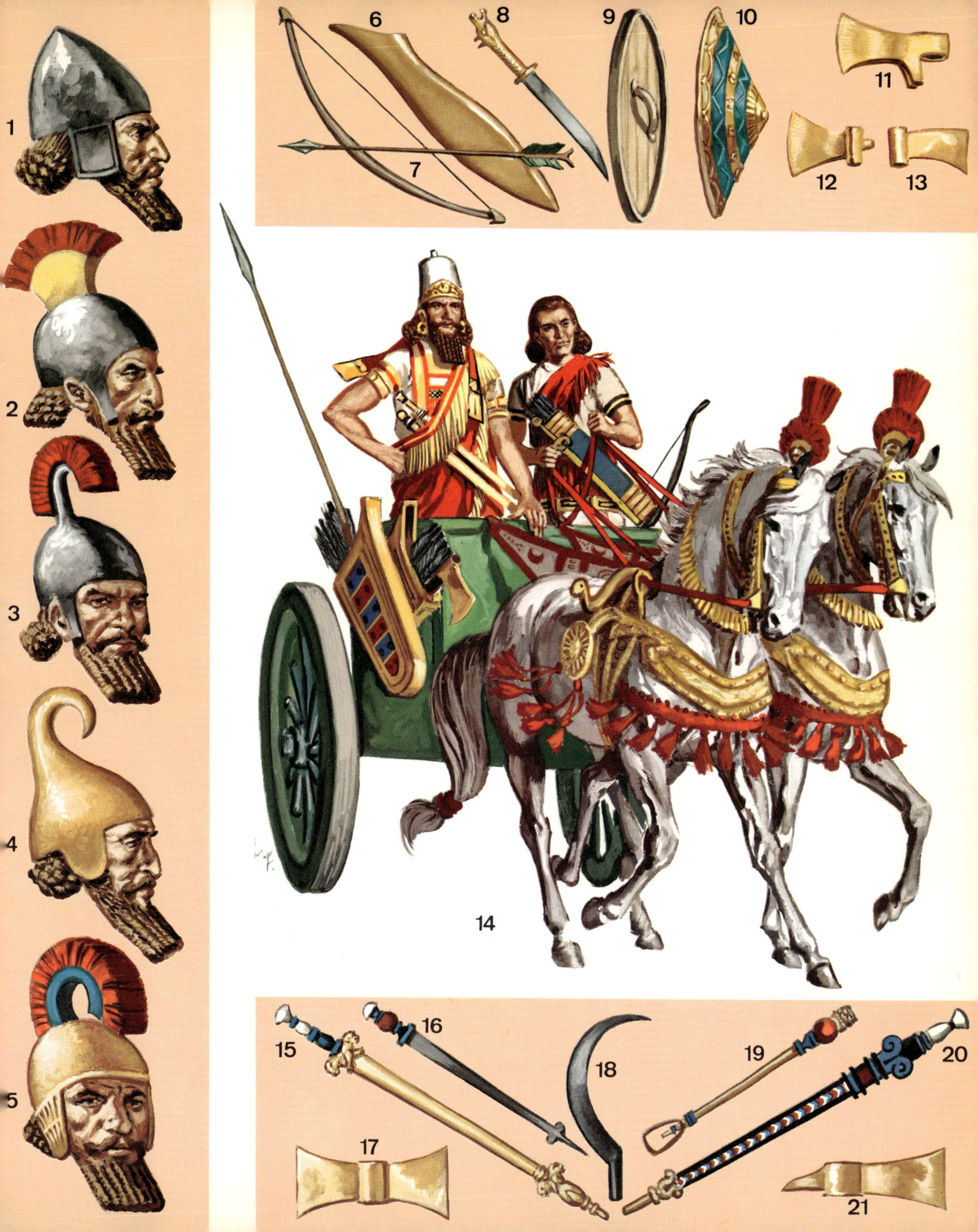
1
2
3
4
5
6
7
8
9
10
11
12
13
14
15
16
17
18
19
20
21

A heavy infantry soldier wore a bronze helmet and his torso was protected by a thick tunic made of material or hide covered with metal plates. His bronze sword hung from a cross-belt and he carried a spear and a leather shield ornamented with metal. The Assyrian soldier showed a surprising piece of vanity; he was particularly attentive to the care of his hair and beard. He parted his hair down the middle, gathered it behind his ears and curled it. He also carefully curled his moustache and beard and applied cosmetics to both. Any warrior who was not well endowed with hair made good the lack with cleverly made hairpieces.

The archers formed a separate corps but, apart from their weapons, they differed little from the pikemen; like them they wore tunics, breeches and leather leg-guards.[1]

The light infantry, who had to be very mobile, did not wear protective jackets, but were armed with javelins or bows. They carried light shields of woven rushes.

Each warrior carried a bladder on his back which he would inflate and use as a float when crossing watercourses. Light boats made of leather waterproofed with tar, forerunners of the assault craft, made it possible to transport small assault groups and chariots.

The cavalry, too, were made up of distinct corps – lancers and archers. It was extremely important because, apart from its role in major actions, it formed the fastest and most mobile combat group in the warfare of surprise strikes. The cavalryman was really a kind of ancient commando. The Assyrian cavalry would infiltrate into enemy territory and clear the way for the main body of the army. They burned villages and terrorised the population deep in the heart of the invaded country. On these raids they carried lightly armed foot-soldiers behind the saddle, an extra load their strong horses bore with ease.[2] Helmeted like the

1, 2, 3, 4, types of Assyrian warriors with their arms; the first wears a long coat of chainmail. 5, Assyrian raiders. 6, 7, 8, three types of javelin. 9, chief's helmet.

[1] p. 19, *3.*   [2] p. 19. *5.*

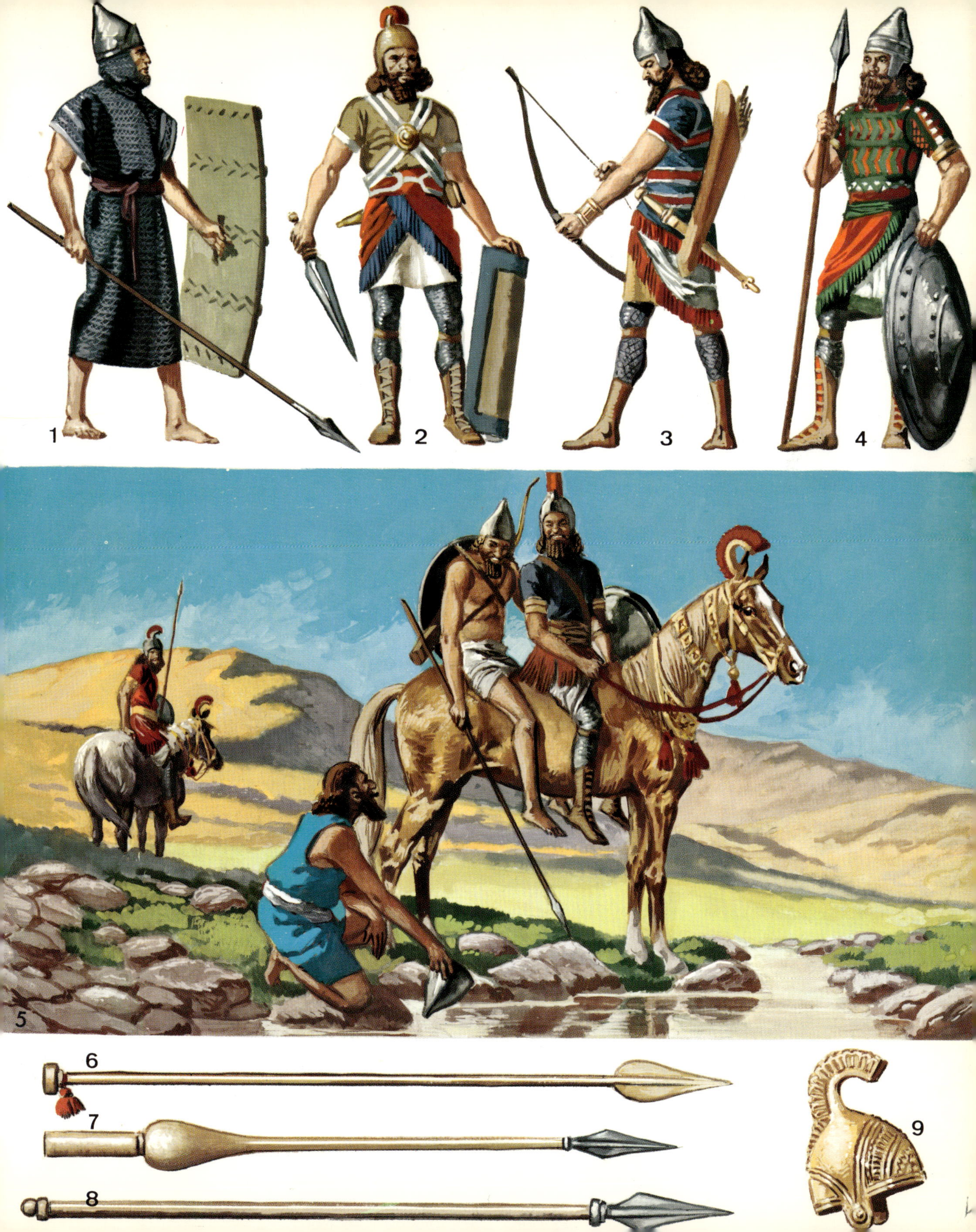
1
2
3
4
5
6
7
8
9

infantry the horsemen rode without saddle, stirrups or spurs; all they had was a blanket. They wore a protective jacket and sometimes breeches, reinforced with metal plates.

A powerful force of chariots came into existence in the 13th century BC. Drawn at first by wild asses; after the domestication of the horse the chariots with their solid wheels became a formidable weapon of conquest. They each carried two or three men armed with javelins and bows, and would thrust deep into the opposing infantry when the latter were unwise enough to advance over open country.

If the enemy took refuge in a fortified town, there were the engineers, who wore stout helmets and long coats of mail. Protected by long bronze shields they drove saps under the walls or dug trenches. If the job proved too difficult for them, siege-engineers could be called up. The giant battering-ram, a huge tree trunk capped with bronze and mounted on wheels, would be used to break down the gates. Mobile siege-towers and scaling ladders would then be brought up against the walls, while crack archers, shielded from head to foot, mowed down the defenders. The Bible mentions Assyrian machines in the 8th Century BC capable of hurling spears and boulders over long distances.

The capture of a town was generally followed by a massacre. The Assyrian knew no pity; indeed he seemed to delight in atrocities. The wretched captives were put to the sword, burned or mutilated. The leaders were flayed alive and their skins hung out on the walls. There was a bounty paid for every enemy head taken and the scribes kept careful account of the gruesome trophies presented to them by the soldiers. Afterwards, as the fancy took them, the conquerors amused themselves in a macabre game of bowls or attached the heads to the vines round about the city.

1, 2, 3, 4, 5, types of harness; 1, is for an emperor's charger. 6, Assyrian chariot; the charioteer wears a protective jacket.

21

Long processions of captives, shackled hand and foot, would then be led off, destined to hard labour in royal building projects. The town would be pillaged from end to end, the booty filling scores of chariots; gold, silver, precious metals, weapons, costly materials and furniture would all be carried off to swell the treasure of Babylon, the 'Gate of God'. But the triumphant king would still not be satisfied. The temples of the vanquished people had to be methodically destroyed, fortifications obliterated, trees cut down and harvests burned.

Assurbanipal himself said: "In a march lasting a month and twenty-five days I devastated the country spreading pain and suffering . . . I silenced the cries of joy in the countryside and left wild asses and gazelles and all manner of wild animals to breed there. . ."

1, mobile assault tower with device for breaking down fortifications. 2, battering-ram. 3, defenders attacking assault tower. 4, archers wearing protective clothing. 5, sappers.

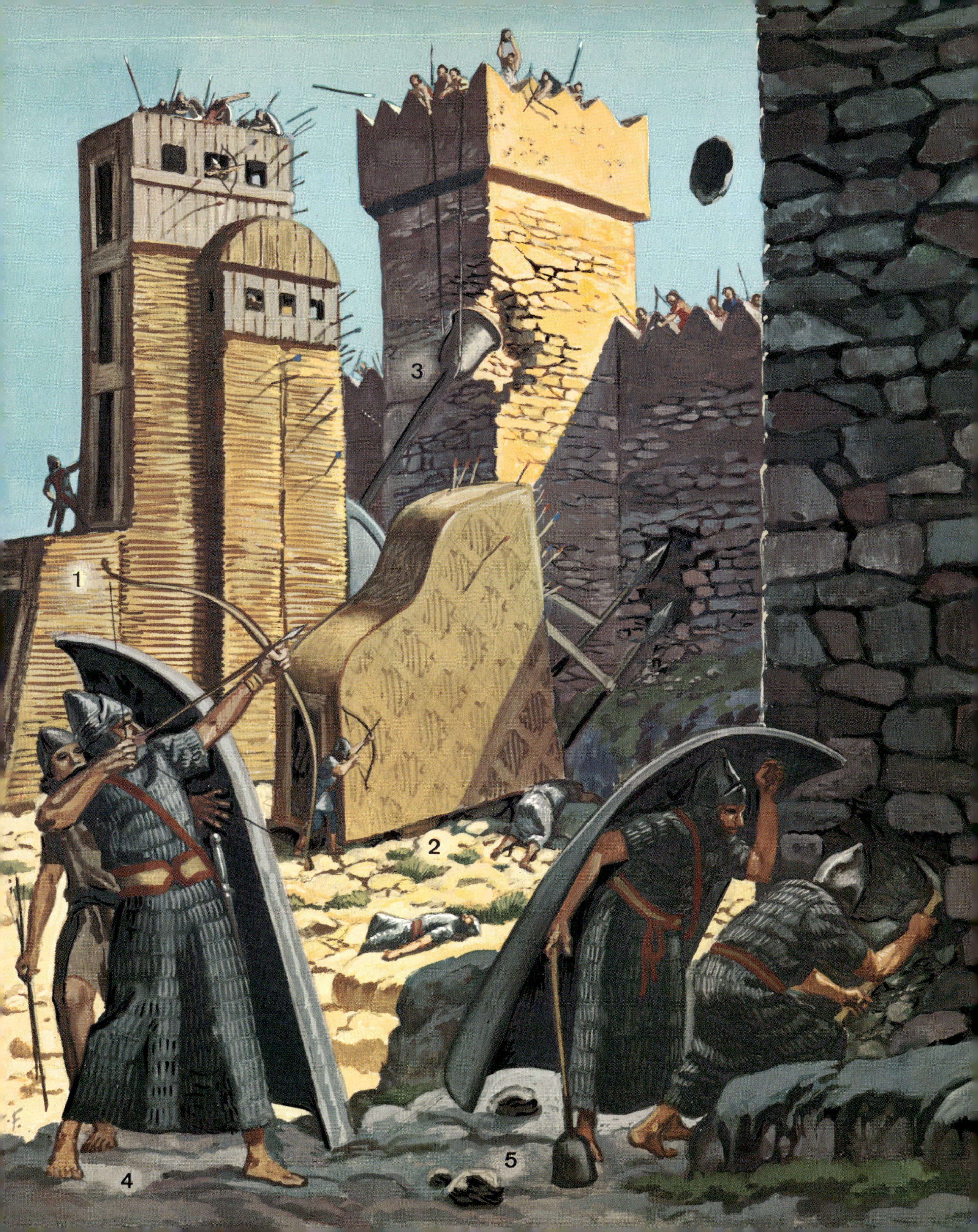
1
2
3
4
5

The Medes and the Persians

While the Assyrian Empire was reaching the height of its power, two white-skinned straight-haired nations, shepherds and cultivators, were settling in the mountains of the plateau of Iran.

The Medes had chosen the north of Iran, and the related Persians the less fertile region along the shores of the Persian Gulf. Being forced to bear the harshness of a climate which, by turns, could be torrid and glacial, these hard-working Aryans became excellent soldiers. All that was needed was a leader to forge them into a race of conquerors.

It was from among the Persians that this leader came. In 549 BC Cyrus imposed his authority on the Medes and Persians and immediately began to prepare his conquest of the east. He built Parsargadae – the camp of the Persians – a fortress and palace surrounded by magnificent gardens. ("Is not Persia the land of flowers, and the rose their queen!") It was from this *paradaiza* – the word still survives in our 'paradise' – that Cyrus set out to conquer a vast empire. He had three powerful men to contend with: Nabonidus, King of Babylon, the Egyptian pharaoh, and the famous and fabulously rich Croesus, King of Lydia. Cyrus decided to attack the Lydians since their treasure was the greatest and gold from the mines of Timolos and nuggets of precious metal from the swift-flowing waters of River Pactolus swelled it constantly.

One summer day, beneath a burning sun, the army began its march on Sardis, the Lydian capital. Most of the infantry wore leather tunics reinforced with scales, breeches and felt or woollen caps called 'tiaras'. Their weapons were the spear, the bow, the mace and the dagger. The Medes' shield, called a 'gerrhe', was of wicker and violin-shaped.[1]

The cavalry carried bows and were mounted on magnificent horses bred in the fertile valleys of Iran. These horses were shod and sometimes they had protective metal plates on the brow and the hocks. There was also a corps of chariots with scythes on the axles and shafts. Lastly – and this was an innovation that was to prove decisive – Cyrus took with him auxiliaries mounted on camels.[2]

The first part of the summer campaign was indecisive. Croesus retreated and waited for the onset of winter, which would halt operations and allow him to raise forces among his Egyptian and

1, unstrung bow. 2, strung bow. 3, strung bow with arrow. 4, 5, the 'Immortals', the personal guard of the Persian kings. 6, sword and scabbard. 7, shield of woven rushes. 8, 9, leather helmets. 10, bronze helmet.

[1] p. 25, *7.* [2] p. 29, *2.*

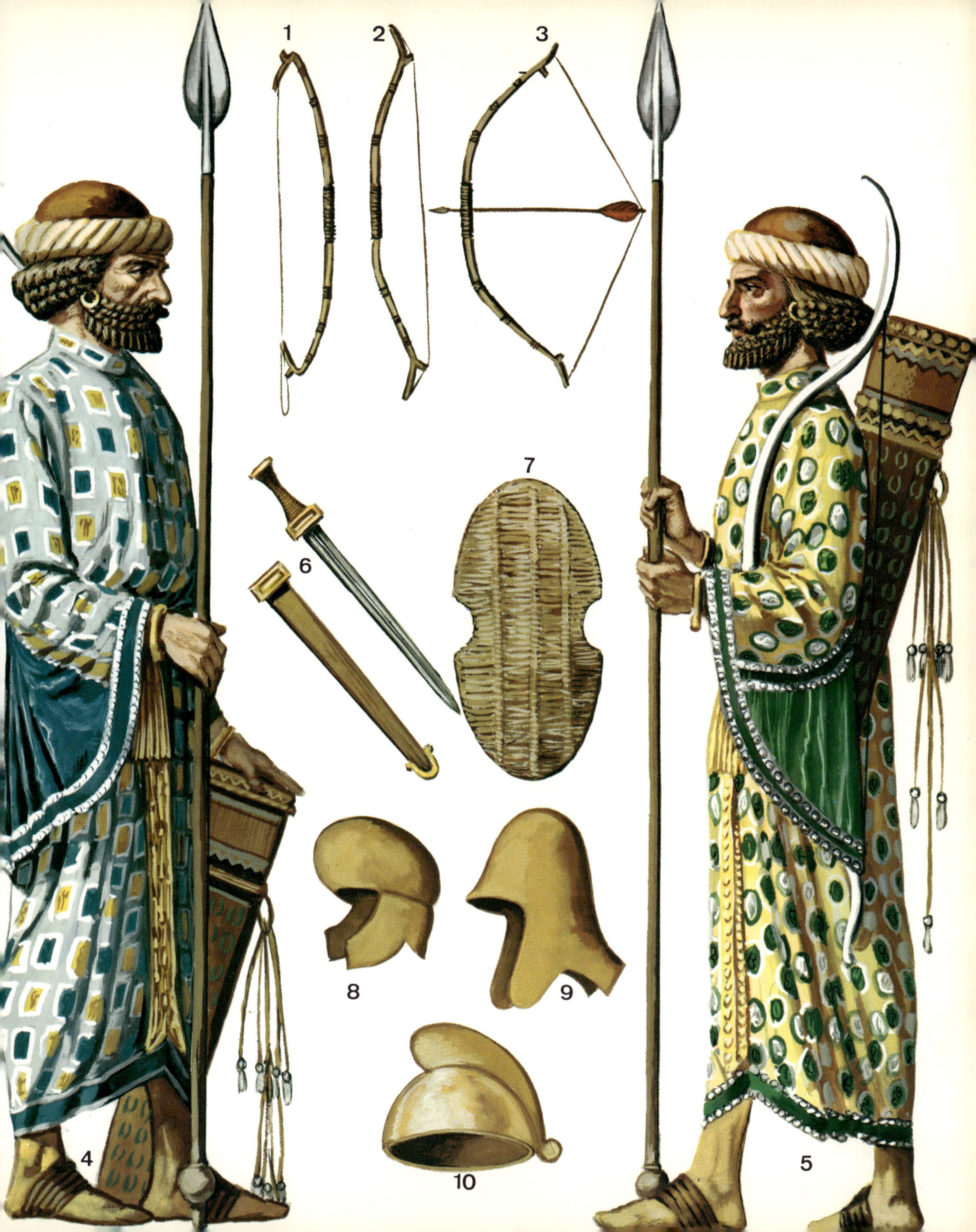
1
2
3
4
5
6
7
8
9
10

Assyrian allies. But Cyrus, ignoring traditional tactics, pressed forward as far as the plain of Thymbrius, in Phrygia, and here Croesus decided to risk a pitched battle.

One of the bloodiest battles of ancient times was about to begin. Worried by the reputation of the brilliant Lydian horsemen, Cyrus resorted to an ingenious strategem. He put his camels in the forefront. They carried on their backs turrets strengthened with iron plates which sheltered two archers. But the General put less reliance on his archers than on the psychological effect of the camels – and their smell! He was not mistaken. The enemy cavalry panicked; his strategem had succeeded. His own chariots then charged and drove a wedge deep into Croesus's army. But Croesus held firm and counter-attacked. Cyrus felt his troops waver and, placing himself at the head of his heavy cavalry, he rode round the enemy's flank and attacked from the rear. At nightfall, the Lydians retreated and took refuge in the fortified city of Sardis, but after a siege of fourteen days it fell. Unlike the Assyrians, Cyrus spared the conquered people and even welcomed Croesus among his own counsellors. The booty was enormous. The wily Cyrus kept it all to himself. His soldiers had to be content with a very modest reward; the Lydians taught them to play dice.

After Lydia it was the turn of the Chaldees. In 539 BC, Cyrus arrived before the gates of Babylon, famous city of the hanging gardens, one of the seven wonders of the world. When evening came, the Persian conqueror stood spellbound before the brightly glittering city with a thousand naptha flares on the ground.

The Prince of Babylon, Belshazzar of the Bible, who was commanding in the absence of his father King Nabonides, remained undismayed. There were provisions in plenty, the garrison was well-manned, and in any case the Euphrates formed an impassable natural obstacle.

Cyrus, however, set about constructing a system of terraces, much to the amusement of the besieged people. Soon, however, their consternation became great, for they saw the water level gradually dropping until the Euphrates was no more than a tiny muddy stream.

Taking up their tools again, the soldiers of Cyrus had altered the course of the river. Babylon was captured and the rest of the Assyrian empire submitted without a fight to the generous and chivalrous conqueror. In 529 BC Cyrus fell in battle while on an

1, Persian officer. 2, Anatolian guard. 3, Persian warrior. 4, Median warrior. 5, standard-bearer. 6, chariot with projecting scythes.

27

expedition against the Scythians from Russia. It was his son, Cambyses, who finished his father's work and conquered Egypt, in 525 BC.

Darius I, who reigned from 521 to 486 BC, extended and organized the Persian empire. His army, made up of nationals augmented with foreign auxiliaries, was reputed to be invincible. The historian Procopius tells of the curious system by which the Persians counted their losses; the army would march past the royal throne and each soldier would drop an arrow into one of the huge baskets set out for the purpose. The baskets were then sealed. At the end of the war, there would be another parade at which each soldier would take an arrow out of the baskets. An officer would then count the number of arrows left over and thus be able to calculate the number of those who had been killed, wounded or taken prisoner. Darius I formed a personal bodyguard, the 'Immortals', an elite corps of about 10,000 men. They wore turbans and costly clothes and were armed with spears, bows and daggers.[1] They were kept up to strength by regular recruitment, losses being immediately replaced.

On his gold and silver throne Darius dreamed of conquering the whole world. The unpredictable Scythians, abandoning Thrace to him, vanished into their endless steppes. The next step was to conquer Greece.

1 p. 25, 4–5.

1, Persian horsemen. 2, war camel. 3, horsemen wearing a protective jacket. 4, Assyrian auxiliary horseman. 5, Phrygian warrior with double-axe, a much-favoured weapon. 6, Scythian horseman. 7, 8, 9, Phrygian warriors. 10, quiver. 11, 12, helmets. 13, shield.

29

4 Greece

At the earliest times the weapons used in Greece were made of bronze. In the 3rd millenium BC, Cretan sailors started importing tin, which when mixed with copper (in the proportion of 1 part in 10) produced the alloy bronze. It continued in use until classical times. Some smelters added other metals, such as lead, calamine,[1] and even silver. The formulae were jealously guarded secrets. One of them – for Corinthian bronze, a particularly brilliant metal – was discovered by pure chance. When Corinth was burned by Mummius in 146 BC objects of bronze, silver and gold, melted in the heat of the brazier flames, produced an alloy so beautiful that the smelters set about reproducing it themselves.

Iron was also known from about 1000 BC, but its use was limited because it was extremely rare; it was, in fact, considered a precious metal. The ancients also knew of steel, an alloy of iron and a small quantity of carbon. The different kinds of steel were tested by being buried in the earth; those that did not rust were recognized as being of the best grade to make the finest weapons. The ancients also knew how to temper steel in water and oil. Homer describes the process in the *Odyssey*. It is also to Homer, in the *Iliad*, that we owe our knowledge of the methods and weapons used in the Trojan War (about 1180 BC).

[1] A sort of zinc.

THE TROJAN HORSE

Slipping quietly from the belly of the famous wooden horse, Ulysses, Tisander, Macaon, Menelaus and many other Greek warriors then opened the gates of Troy to the Greek army. King Priam's proud city was destroyed and never rebuilt. The warrior standing beside the brazier is wearing a helmet decorated with pig's teeth.

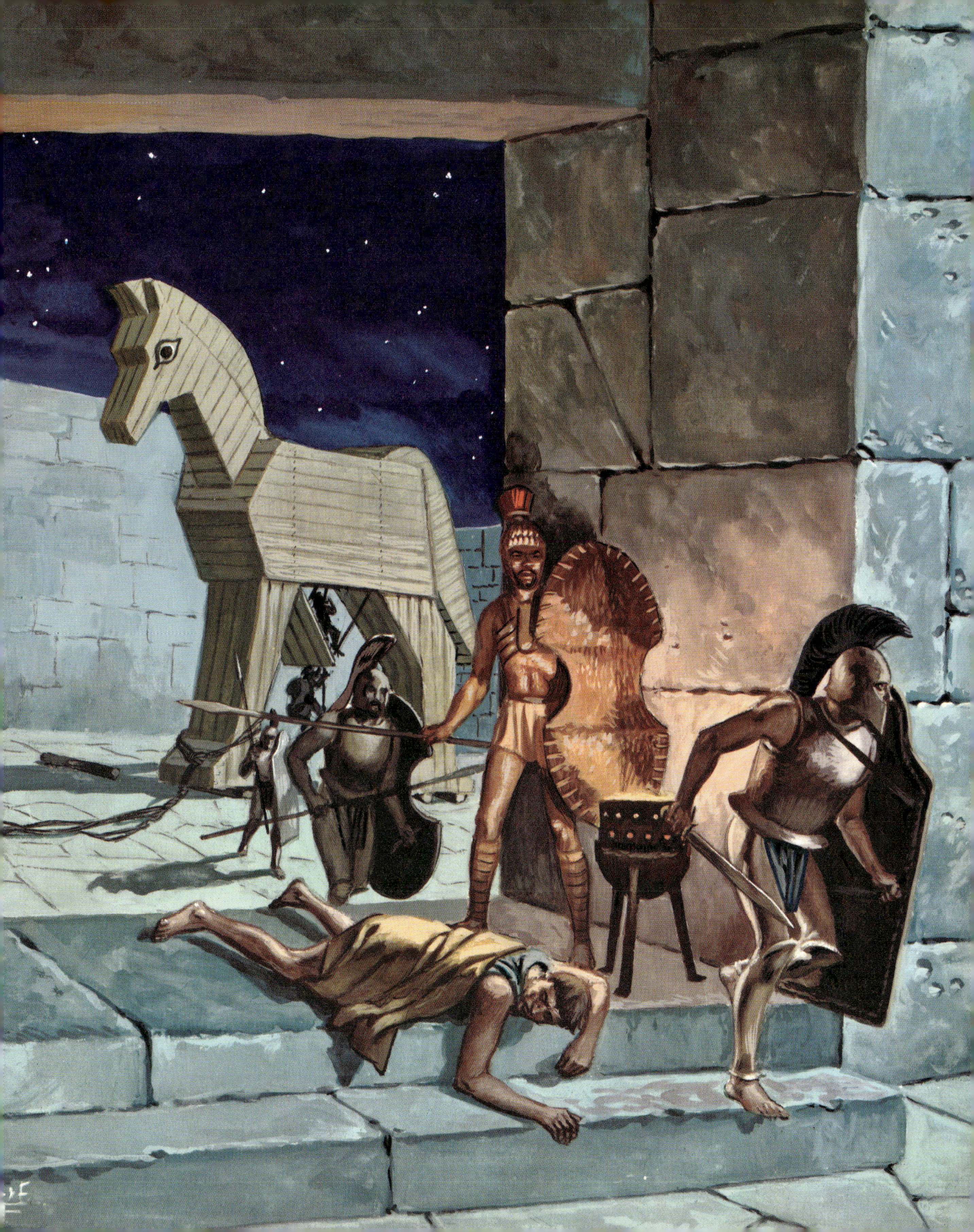

The many representations of the Trojan heroes by the late Greek artists are of no significance as a record of the age to which they refer. On the other hand, they are a full and precise record of the military costumes of their own times.

The Homeric heroes had the following defensive equipment: helmets, body armour, shield and greaves. The helmet was usually of bronze and had a visor, a projection at the back to protect the neck and a crest with a plume or long mane. One type of helmet, described by Homer as being made of boars' tusks, was a source of mystery to classical scholars until, one day, during the excavation of a tomb, archaeologists discovered a helmet carrying a parallel row of tusks.[1]

The body armour consisted of a jerkin of leather or strips of strengthened material. On this the passages in Homer seem to refer to a later date and are not reliable evidence.

The shield was long, often covering the soldier from head to foot. It was also used as a bed and a stretcher. Another kind of shield, typical of this period, was in the form of a figure '8'. It was very much lighter and accounts for the wounds to the thighs and sides sustained by the heroes of the *Iliad*.[2]

GREEK HELMETS

1a and 1b, two positions in which the Doric helmet was worn. 2, Greek helmet without nose guard. 3, Italo-Greek helmet. 4, Corinthian helmet. 5, Attic helmet with cheek-guards. 6, Boeotian helmet, one of the commonest types. 7, Corinthian helmet. 8, 4th century BC helmet.

[1] p. 31, centre. [2] The 2 types of shield are shown on p. 31.

32

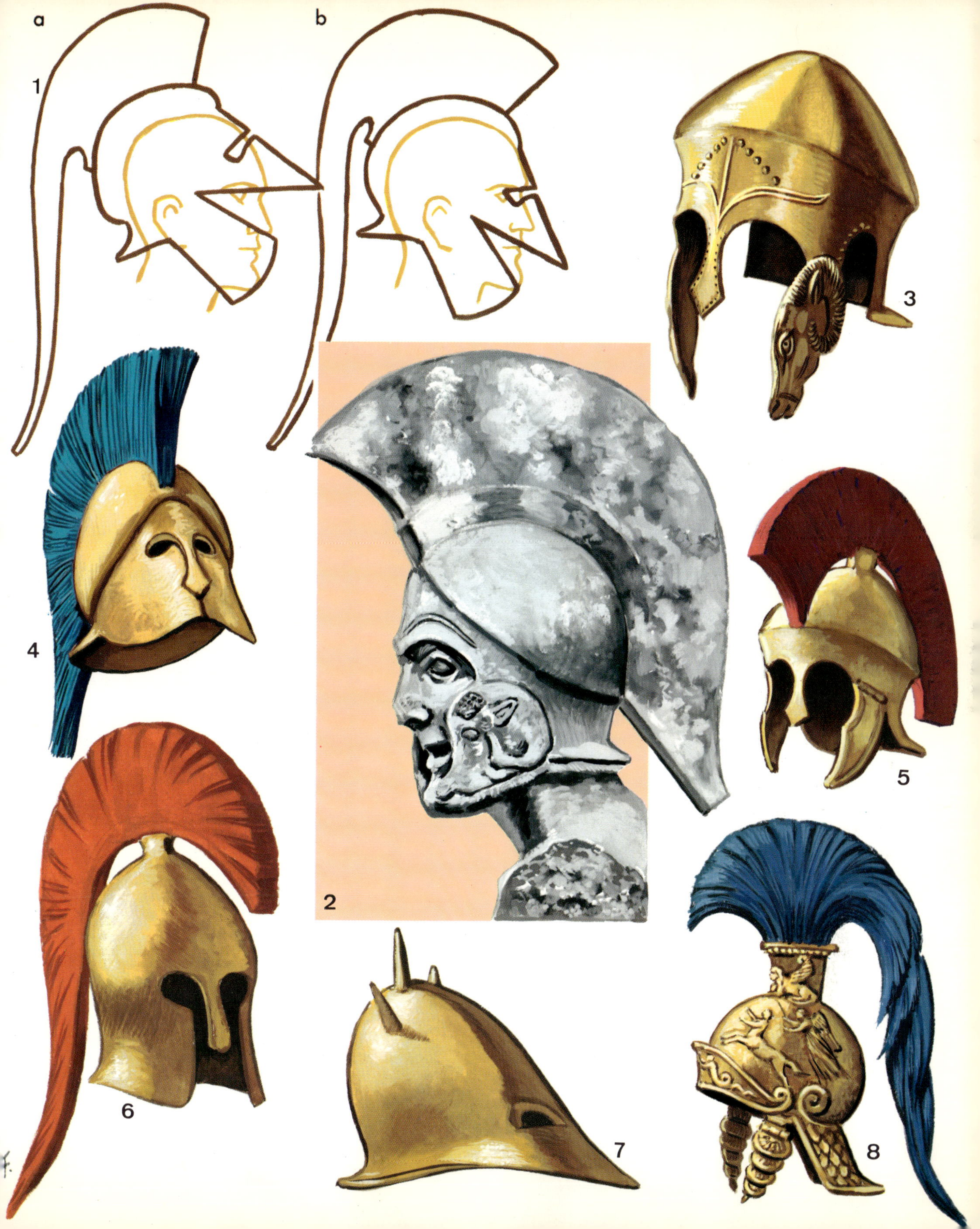
a
b
1
2
3
4
5
6
7
8

Greaves completed the defensive equipment. They were made of bands of material or leather secured with buckles. For persons of high rank, the buckles were of precious metal. Sandals were worn. The offensive weapons consisted mainly of a spear with a small ridged head rounded towards the socket[1] and a short sword or dagger – the 'parazonium'.

Greek warriors of this epoch used chariots but seem to have preferred fighting on foot to merely throwing a few javelins before getting out of the vehicle. They seem not to have used cavalry in battle.

The ordinary foot-soldiers, lowly followers of the Homeric heroes, had little protective equipment. They carried a light wooden shield and javelins and hurled stones from wooden slings. Homer's heroes disliked the sling, but excelled at throwing stones by hand. Like ten-pin bowlers they knocked away the enemy's shields by hurling the largest stones they could carry. Discus throwing was excellent training for this form of combat!

The bow, judged unworthy to be used by a hero, was left to the lesser men. If Paris or Tencros did occasionally condescend to use the bow it was only to display their outstanding skill. Aeneas, seeing all ranks of the Trojans mowed down by Diomedes, called

[1] The socket was partly hollowed out to take the shaft.

RETREAT OF THE TEN THOUSAND

Fourteen thousand Greek mercenaries, to whom history has given the name of the 'Ten Thousand', had just fought in the victorious army of Cyrus the Younger, who was trying to depose his brother Artaxerxes II from the Persian throne. When Cyrus was killed at the battle of Cunaxa, on the Euphrates (401 BC), his Persian troops dispersed, and the Greeks, led by the Athenian Xenophon, began their dangerous retreat. In his book *Anabasis* Xenophon describes the difficulties and miseries the Greeks had to endure in the course of their long trek from the Euphrates to the Black Sea. Our picture shows them crossing the mountains of Armenia in a freezing December wind.

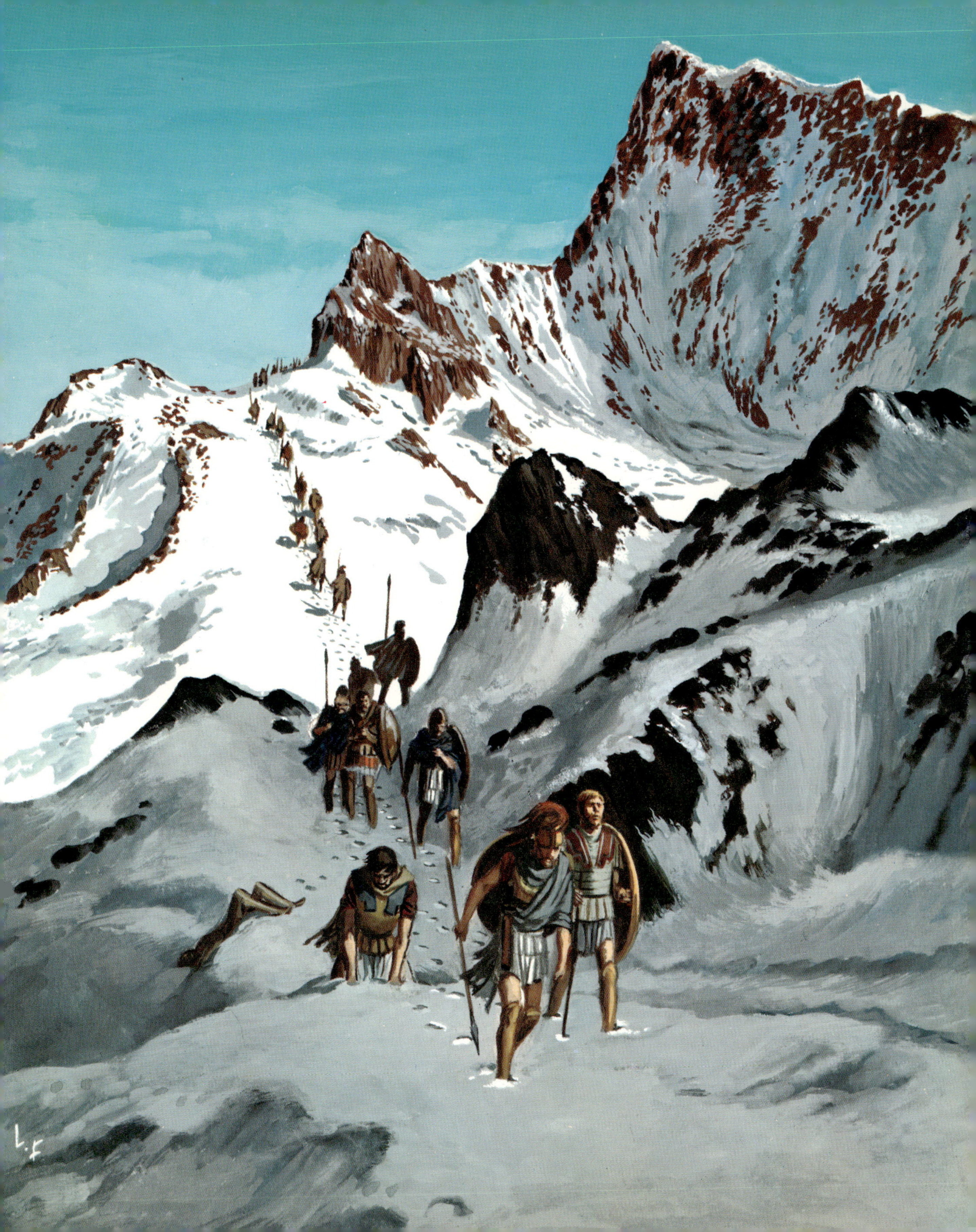

upon the divine Pandarus. 'Pandarus, where are your bow and arrow? Hurl your shafts upon the unknown hero. See how he triumphs!'

There were, of course, a number of general frays, but it is remarkable how often encounters between the two sides took the form of single combat. Throughout the Homeric poems we see two heroes confronting one another. They talk together, taunt and hurl insults at each other, while all the time each is watching for the moment when the opponent is distracted or unnerved to make a sudden thrust with his spear; this shows how effective the shield could be.

The spears were constantly in motion: the warriors feinted, ducked behind their shields, raised them, then lowered them. Clearly one's strength had to match the length of one's tongue! Sooner or later the left arm of one of them would tire, his reflexes would get slower, and he was doomed.

About 650 BC, there were great changes in the equipment and tactics used by the Greek warriors. From that time the soldier appears to us in a familiar form, the hoplite. The defensive equipment was the helmet, body armour, shield and greaves.

The helmet, of which there were many designs, was made of bronze and had a crest with a plume or a horsehair mane. The oldest helmet was the Corinthian, also called the 'Minervan'. This was

HELMETS, WEAPONS AND GREAVES

1, 2, 3, 4, 7, light infantry helmets. 5, triple-crested Corinthian helmet. 6, helmet with visor in the shape of a face with hair and beard (5th century BC). 8a and 8b, greave seen from front and back. 9, peltaste's leg-guard and sandal. 10, hoplite's shoe. 11, sandal and greave of leather.

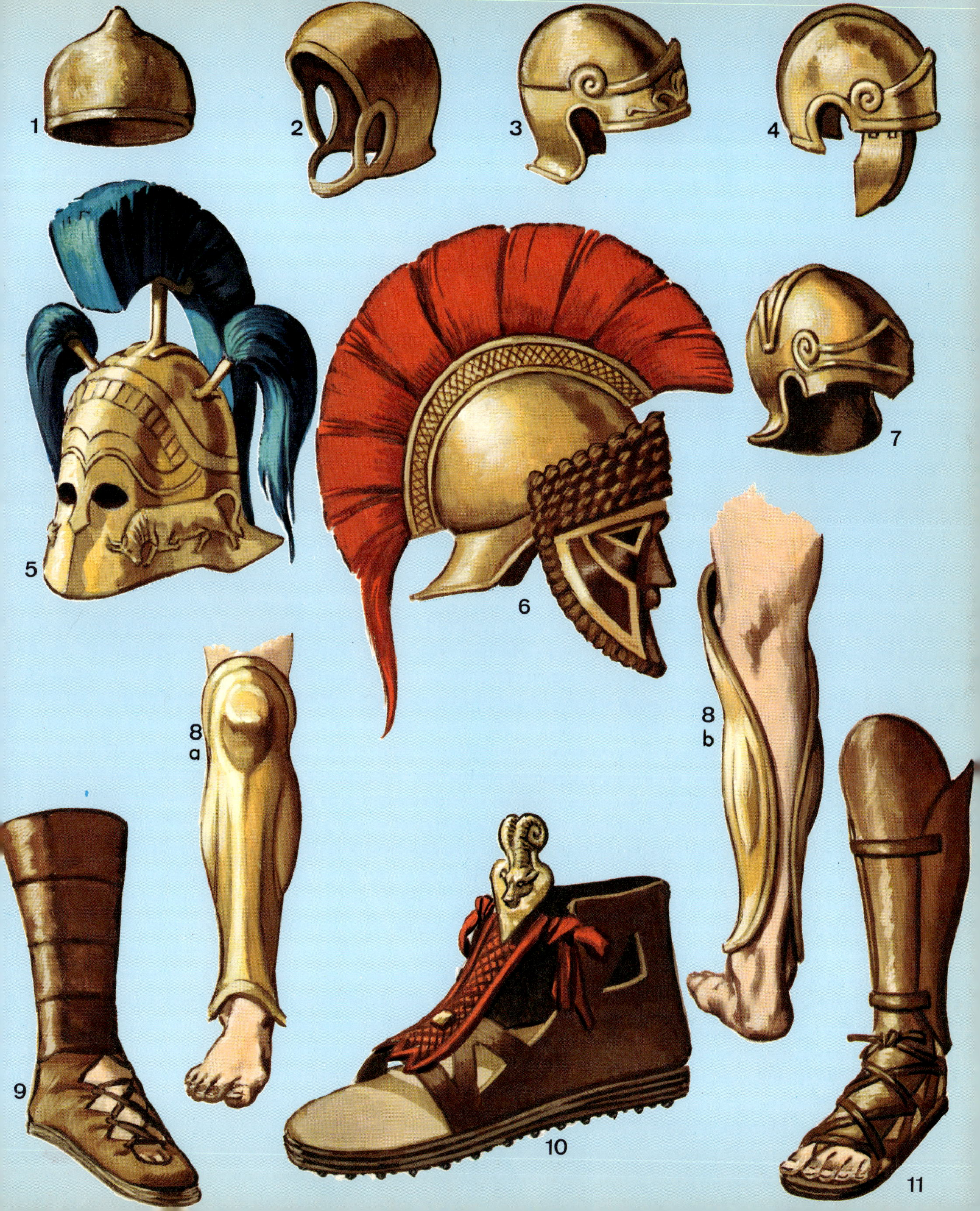
1
2
3
4
5
6
7
8
a
8
b
9
10
11

in the form of a mask and came down below the chin.[1] The Dorian helmet had a large visor.[2] The Attic helmet had hinged projections over the cheeks[3] which the soldiers could lower when in action. Sometimes the head piece had a projection over the nose but, more often, there was an extension at the back to protect the neck.

Why do we find so many different designs of helmet among the same body of hoplites? It is because these soldiers often had to equip themselves at their own expense, and so it was thought reasonable not to make them bear the added expense of providing equipment of a uniform design.

The bronze breastplate[4] was made of two convex plates, and some have survived to the present day. Frequent mention is made of protective garments made of leather, of metal scales or of reinforced material, the latter providing protection against animal bites. Metal was very much sought-after. It was used in the form of plates sewn on to leather, preparing the way for the breastplate with shoulder pieces and martlets. It was made of a corselet, metal plates over the shoulders and strips of leather over the stomach. This armour was worn over a red tunic.[5]

The circular shield measured about 1 m/3 ft across. It was often made entirely of metal, sometimes of several thicknesses of cowhide sewn together and covered with metal plates. The front was

THE PASS OF THERMOPYLAE

Leonidas, King of Sparta, was holding in check the massive army of Xerxes, who was trying to force the pass of Thermopylae (480 BC). A traitor named Ephialtes showed the Persians a secret route and they surprised the Greeks from the rear. Forewarned, Leonidas sacrificed himself and his three hundred Spartans to cover the retreat of the main part of the Greek army.

1 p. 33, *4/6*; p. 37, *5.* 2 p. 33, *1.* 3 p. 33, *5.* 4 p. 39, p. 41, *4.* 5 p. 41, *1–5.*

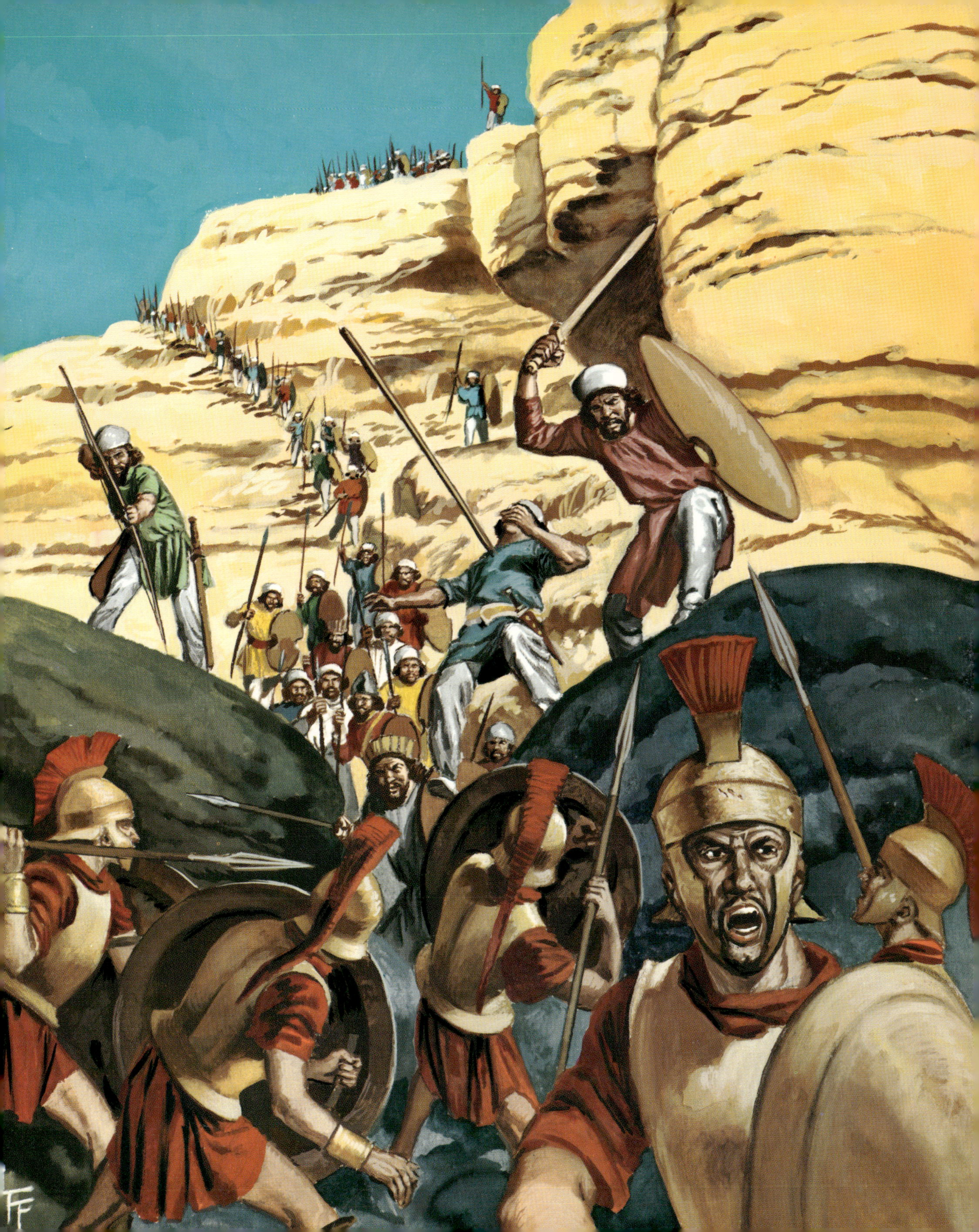

decorated with traditional figures and emblems intended to ward off bad luck. Some shields, in addition, had a sort of fringed apron to break the impact of arrows and blows; they also bore the insignia of the bearer's unit.

At the beginning bronze or pewter greaves were a normal part of the hoplite's equipment. They were made individually for each warrior, fitting close to the legs thanks to their moulded form and the pliability of the metal. On his feet the hoplite wore strong studded sandals or 'crepides'.[1]

As offensive weapons, the hoplite carried the spear, sword and parazonium. The spear-shaft was of ash and over 2 metres long. The head was leaf-shaped. In the 4th Century BC, Philip of Macedon armed his hoplite phalanxes with the 'sarissa', a spear reputed to have been over 7 m/23 ft long. The historian Polybius mentions a length of from 8 to 9 m/26 to 29 ft.

The sword was quite short and hung from a belt on the left side. The solid hilt was riveted on.[2] The parazonium[3] hung from the belt on the right side.

From the beginning of the 4th Century BC, the light infantry carried the 'pelta', a small shield of wood or wicker covered with leather.[4]

1 p. 37. 10   2 p. 51, *14–15*.   3 p. 51, *13*.   4 p. 51, *2–3*.

HOPLITES

1, 2, 3, 4, 5, hoplites. 1, and 5, have the cheek-guards of their helmets raised. 3, is wearing leather body armour. 4, has a bronze cuirass of early style. The head in the background is of Alexander the Great (356–323 BC).

40

1

2

3

4 5

The 'peltastes' formed an immediate group between the hoplites and the 'psiletes', who had no defensive equipment. The psiletes were divided into 'toxotes' or archers, 'sphendonetes' or slingers, and 'acontistes' or javelin-throwers.

The Greek cavalry was not formed until the middle of the 5th Century BC. It was not in evidence at the battle of Marathon (490 BC) or later at Plataeus, but then the exploits of the Persian cavalry during the wars against the Medes inspired the Greeks to form a cavalry arm. The Athenian cavalry started with 300 men but later the strength rose to more than 1,000. When the Peloponnesian war broke out, it stood at 1,200 of whom 200 were archers. The cavalry were recruited from among the two upper classes of citizens. With neither stirrups nor horse shoes with calkins the horseman could only charge the enemy at the risk of being thrown from his mount. His job was limited to harassing the enemy and showering him with javelins, which were, with the sword, his main offensive weapons. The defensive equipment of the cavalry consisted of the helmet (Xenophon greatly admired the Boeotian), body armour and the shield.[1]

In Greece, horse-breeding was a hit and miss affair. They made up for the weakness of the hoofs by hardening the horn with pitch or fitting iron shoes called 'hipposandals' that were attached to the pastern by straps.

1 p. 43 & 45.

THE BATTLE OF ISSUS

The first encounter between Alexander and Darius took place at Issus, in Cilicia, 333 BC. The Greek cavalry played a decisive part in the battle.

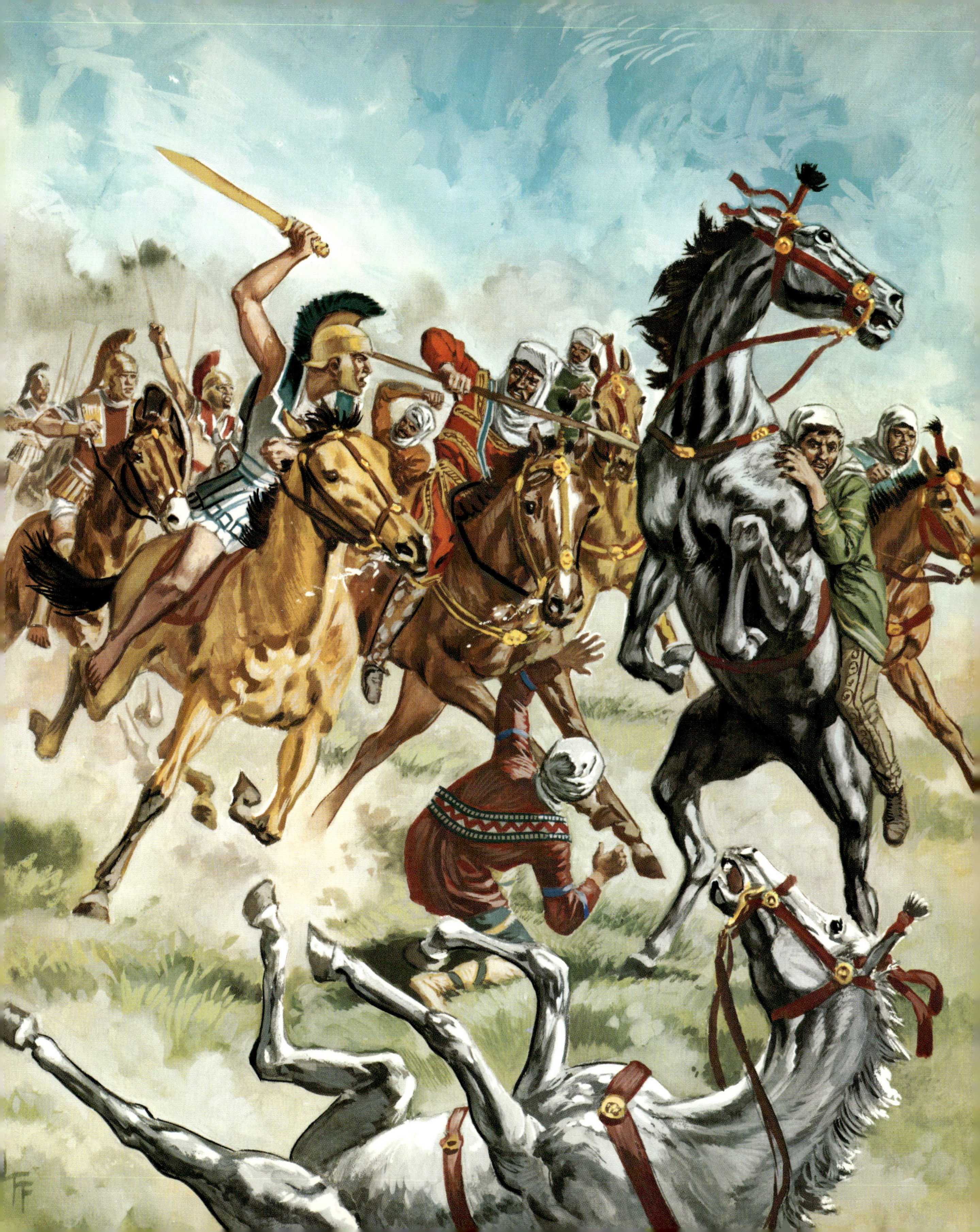

In battle, the various corps that we have just described formed the phalanx, in which everything was calculated to produce its effect by weight of numbers.[1] The simple phalanx in battle array comprised the heavy infantry of hoplites (4,096 men) in the centre flanked by two battalions of light infantry (each of 1,024 men). The two wings were made up of cavalry; each of them had 8 squadrons of 64 horsemen – an overall strength of 7,168.

The hoplites were drawn up in 16 ranks of 256 men; the light infantry in 8 ranks of 128. Each squadron of cavalry formed a square 8 ranks of 8.

Four phalanxes formed an army, and was called a tetraphalanx.

As the order of battle of the tetraphalanx finally developed the separate phalanxes were deployed in an entirely different way from the one we have just described.

Hoplites formed the front line in four equal masses. The light infantry formed a second line behind the hoplites, and the cavalry were on the wings.

The successors of Alexander the Great placed war elephants[2] in the intervals between the groups of infantry. Alexander had captured five from Darius after the battle of Arbela, in 331 BC, but had wisely decided to use them only as beasts of burden because in

1 See diagrams on p. 49. 2 p. 47.

44

GREEK CAVALRY
1, chariot. 2, epitagmarch. 3, milarch. 4, mounting with the aid of a cross-piece fixed to a spear. 5, horseman.

45

battle they had been known to turn against their own side, as we shall see later on in our chapter on the Roman armies.

The tetraphalanx numbered 16,384 hoplites, 8,192 peltastes and 4,096 cavalry: a total of 28,672 men.

Deployed in ranks 16 deep the hoplites had a 'lochages' or file-leader in the front rank, a 'dimoerites' or half-file leader in the ninth and an 'ouragos' or serrefile leader in the sixteenth.

If we accept the length of the 'sarissa' given by Polybius – 14 to 16 cubits, or 8–9 m/26–30 ft – the front rank of the phalanx presented to the enemy a line of spearheads projecting some 6 m/19½ ft, a second one projecting some 5 m/16½ ft, a third some 4 m/13 ft, a fourth some 3 m/9½ ft, a fifth some 2 m/6½ ft, and a sixth about 1 m/3 ft. In this way, each file presented spearheads, each 1 m/3 ft behind the other. Nothing could resist the impact of such a body of men, so long as it held its formation.[1]

The next ten ranks, reduced to a passive role at the beginning of any action, held their 'sarissae' forward and slightly tilted so as to disperse the ensuing flights of arrows, in a forest of spears. These rear ranks also prevented the front ranks from giving an inch of ground; in fact, they would remorselessly force them forward.

BATTLE ELEPHANTS

In 280 BC, Pyrrhus, the King of Epirus defeated the Romans near Heraclea, in Lucania. For a long time, the battle hung in the balance but finally victory went to the Greeks, thanks to their battle-elephants.

1 p. 49, *4*.

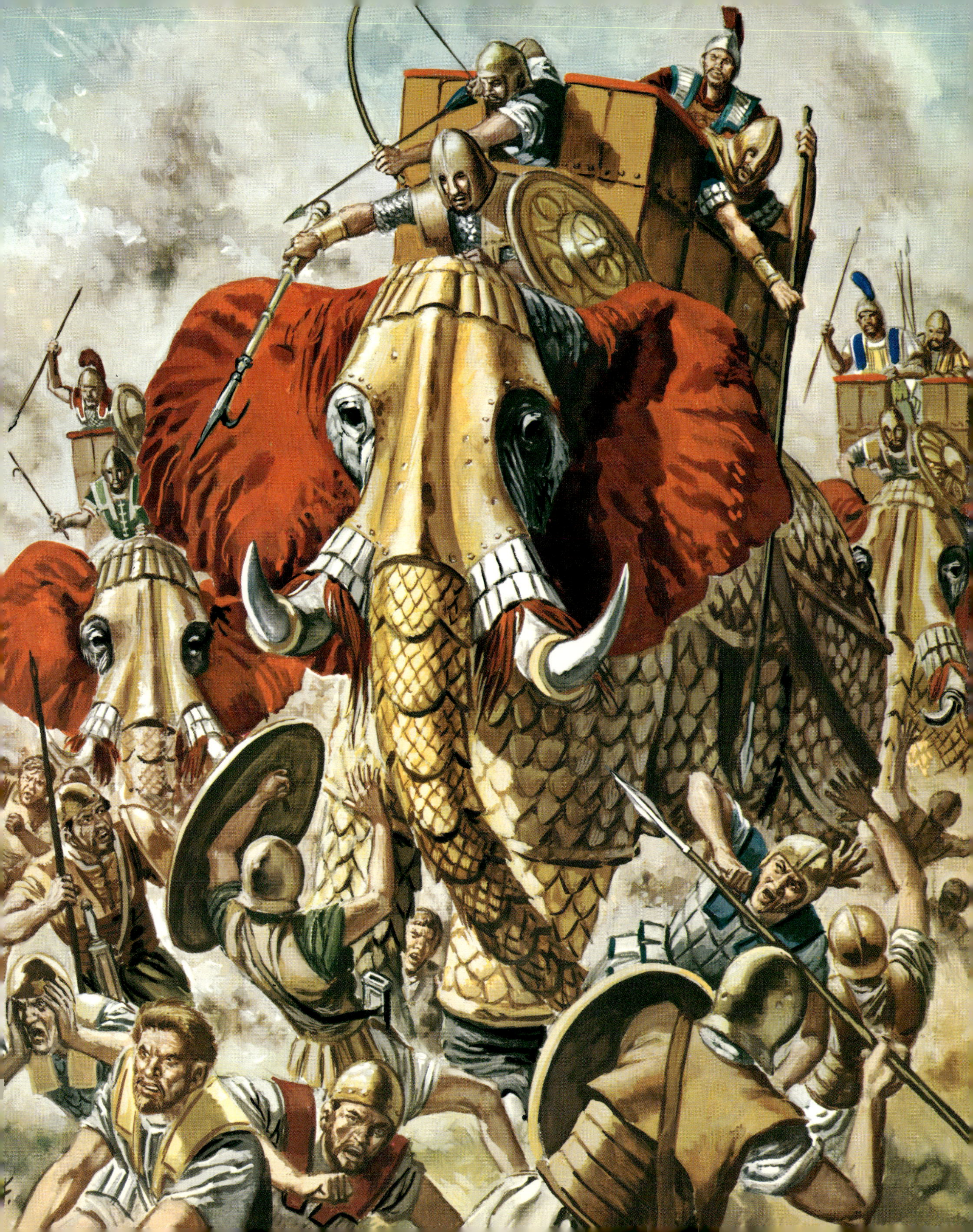

The tetraphalanx included 64 standard-bearers, one to each 'xenagy' or tetrarchy of 64 men, a trumpeter, a sergeant-major, a connecting file, and an orderly whose duty it was to transmit the orders of the commanders.

Before Alexander's time, armies marched and manoeuvred to the sounds of the flute. Later it was replaced by the trumpet, particularly where dust or mist obscured visual signals. The strictest silence was observed in the ranks, even at the height of battle. The sight of this mass of men charging in complete silence must have been terrifying. The consul Paulus Emilius (216 BC) had to admit his fright when he saw these awesome phalanxes for the first time, though in the end his own legions defeated them.

The orders of command were like those of today. 'Listen for the order,' ('Watch your front'), 'Take up your positions,' ('Fall in'), 'Straighten the lines,' ('Right dress'), 'Shoulder arms,' 'To the spear (i.e. right) turn,' 'To the shield (i.e. left) turn,' and so on.

The Greeks were careful to keep their orders concise. To indicate the direction of a movement they used the preliminary words of command 'in the Laconian way' or 'in the Macedonian way,' so that soldiers might know whether they were to advance or retreat. Some Greek generals became famous for their skill at improvization. Unconquered on so many battlefields, the phalanx finally suffered defeat at the hands of the invading Romans.

THE TACTICS OF THE PHALANX

1, the phalanx: a, hoplites; b, light infantry; c, cavalry. 2, the light infantry (b) advances and attacks with arrows and javelins. 3, the light infantry (b) reforms behind the hoplites (a) while the cavalry (c) wheels to encircle the enemy. 4, hoplites mounting six banks of spears. 5, the tetraphalanx. Hoplites (a) form the front line, the light infantry (b) the second. The battle-elephants are posted at (d).

1

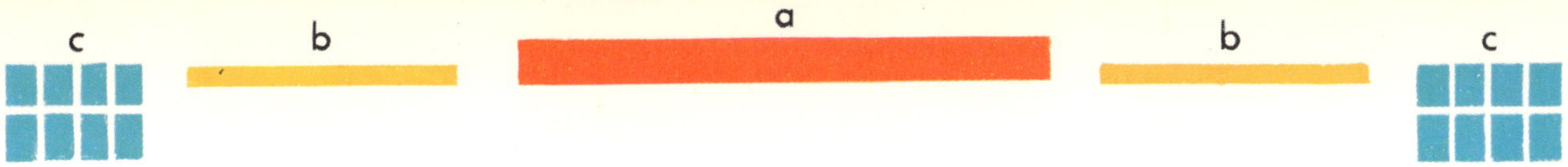

2

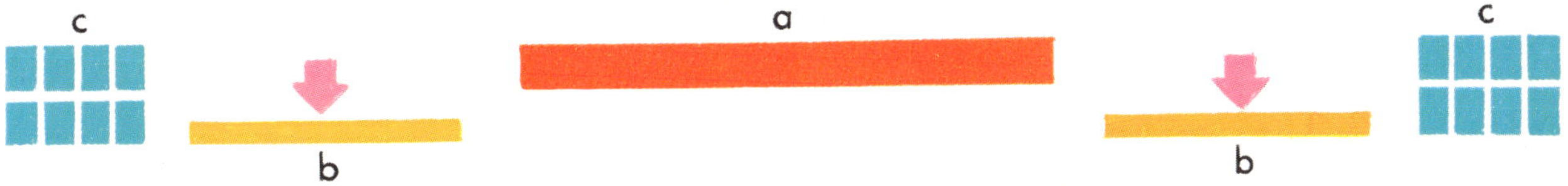

3

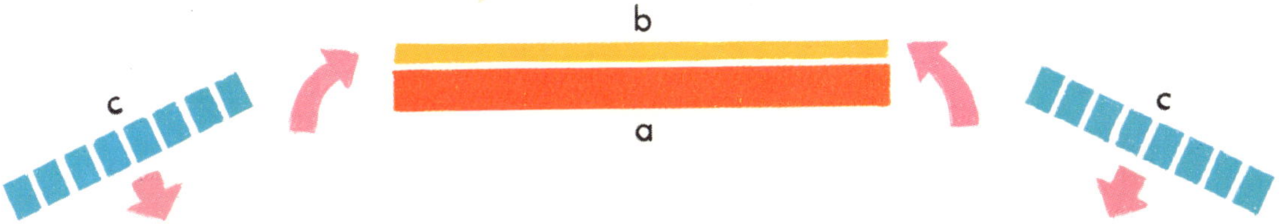

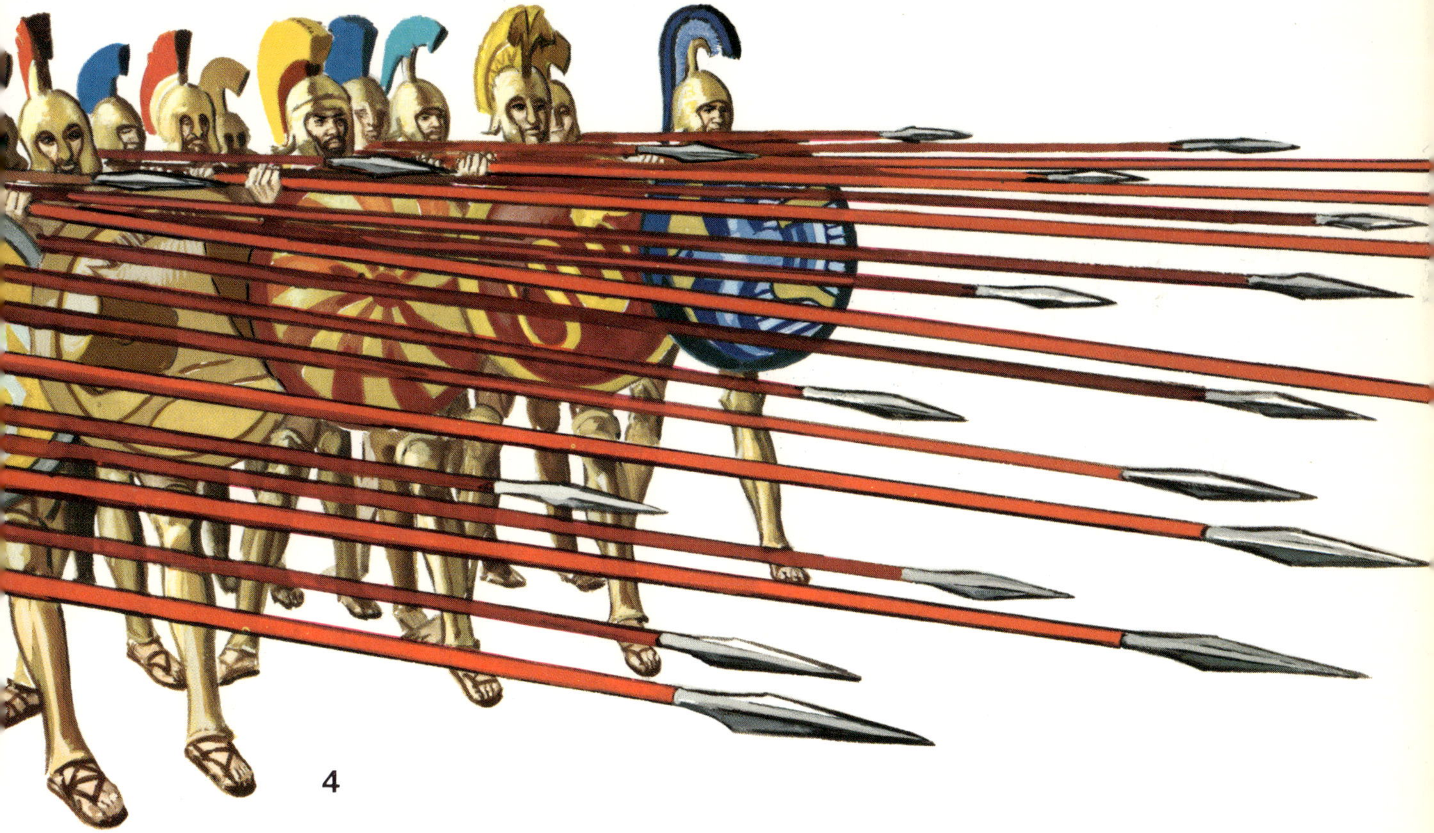

4

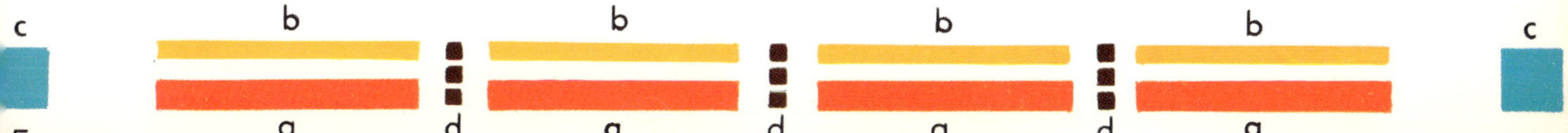

5

Polybius gives us the reasons for this defeat. To be at its most effective the phalanx could fight in only one place at one time and in one way. It required a flat open country without ditches, swamps, gullies, slopes or rivers. The Romans were careful not to risk themselves on such ground; they scattered through the countryside ravaging towns and cutting supply lines. If the phalanx sought out the enemy on their ground, it met only a fraction of the opposing forces, the remainder being held in reserve. Whether the phalanx managed to break the enemy line or its own line was broken, whether it pursued the fleeing enemy or was itself pursued, the outcome was that its ranks broke and it lost its fighting efficiency so that the Roman reserves launching themselves against the breaches in the line, attacked not the front, but the flank or the rear. For a long time the Greeks believed that the Romans had only defeated them by a fluke. They never understood how the Roman formation had managed to triumph over their invincible phalanxes.

GREEK SOLDIERS

1, archer wearing a helmet in the form of an animal's head. 2, Thracian peltaste wearing a linen cuirass and carrying the small shield called a 'pelta'. 3, peltaste with two-ended spear. 4, hoplite armed with a type of sabre. 5, 7, 8, military musicians. 6, Scythian mercenary archer of the Athenian police. 9, 10, 11, 12, early spearheads. 13, dagger where blade is riveted to the hilt. 14, 15, swords. 16, axe-head.

51

The Etruscans

By the 7th Century BC the Etruscans had established a flourishing empire in Italy. They are a mysterious people. We know neither what race they belonged to nor their language. We do know they were sturdy and thick-set, and that they spread to Latium and founded the city of Capua in Campania.

As a result of close contact with the Greek colonies in the south of Italy, the Etruscans adopted their weapons, with slight modifications. Their skilled craftsmen copied wholesale the Greek objects of art and pottery. They were good architects, and they built towns with considerable ramparts.

Between the Etruscans and the Greeks lived four distinct groups – the Umbrians, the Sabines, the Samnites and the Latins. They occupied the plain of the Tiber, or Latium, and the Abruzzi mountains. While the isolated mountain-dwellers had long preserved their primitive customs, the inhabitants of the plain learned a great deal from their contact with strangers. They quickly established themselves into a single nation that became Rome. The Romans soon attacked the Etruscan Empire, already exposed to the incursions of the Gauls, and it finally went under with the capture of Bologna in 350 BC.

ETRUSCAN SOLDIERS

1, officer. 2, spear-man with body armour reinforced with bronze scales. 3, soldier wearing the classical Greek body armour. 4, 5, soldiers wearing cuirasses. The early shields were often beautifully embossed. 6, the cowl-shaped helmet is similar to that worn by some Roman gladiators. 7, archer, light troops. 8, Samnite warrior from the mountains of central Italy.

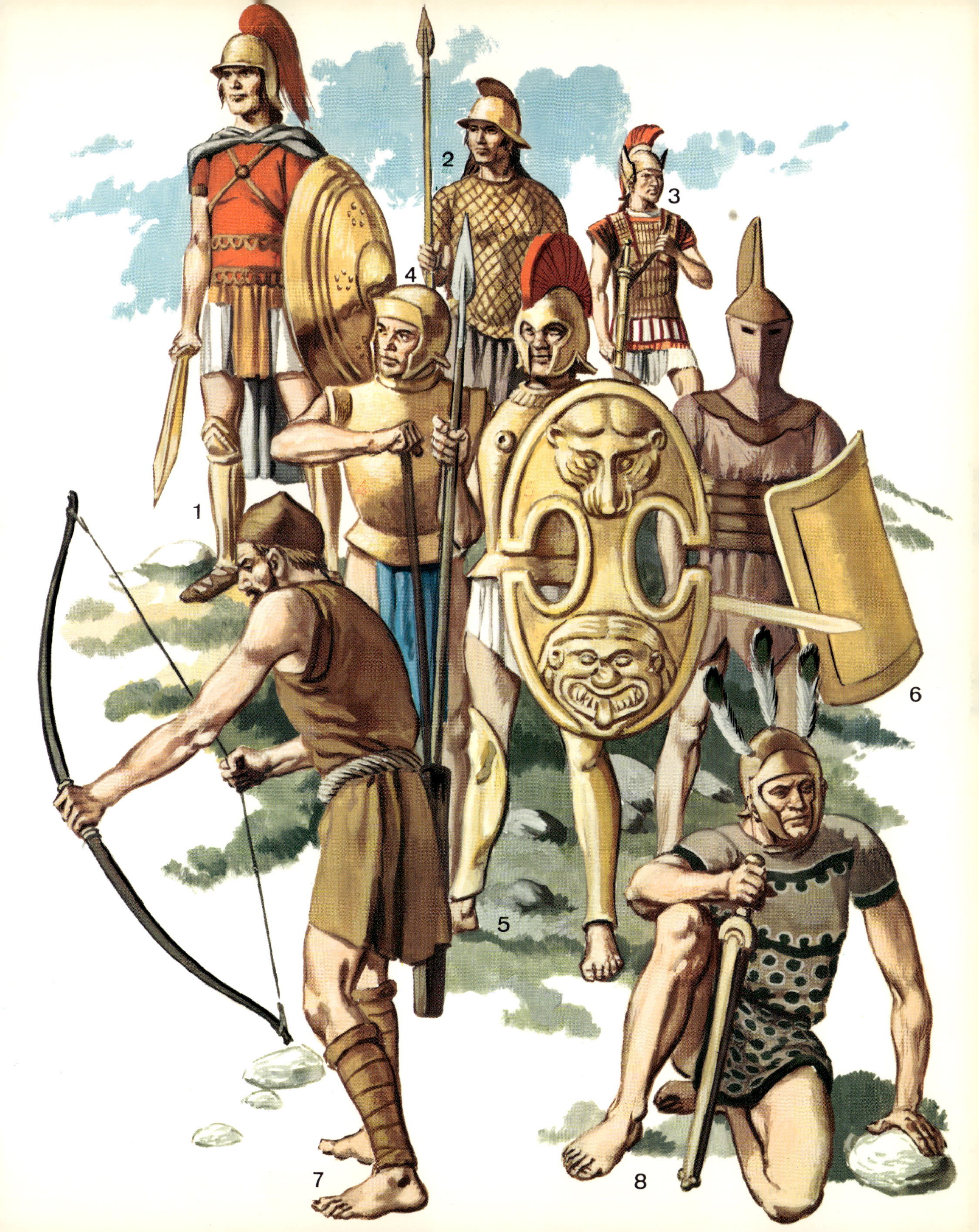
1
2
3
4
5
6
7
8

Rome

The story of the origins of Rome has come down to us only through the works of the historian Livy, who wrote during the time of the emperor Augustus. Livy's extravagant pride in his country makes him a very biased witness.

Very little is known about the earliest army which was known as the Army of Servius.

The first kings of Rome had at their disposal 3,000 infantry (milites) and 300 cavalry (celeres). The word 'legio' (legion) from 'legere', meant levy and seems to have designated the whole body of armed forces.

In the legions of Servius, the citizens ranked according to their wealth. The richest served in the cavalry, the less rich in the heavy infantry, and so on down to the fifth and poorest class, who were relegated to the ancillary services.

In the 4th Century BC, military operations dragged on and prevented the demobilization of the legion, so the dictator Camillus introduced regular pay for the army. He divided the legion into three tactical groups: 'hastatii', 'principes' and 'triarii'. The light infantry, 'velites' recruited from the people, were a separate body.

The 'hastatii'[1] were recruited only from among the young men. The name comes from their long spear, 'hasta'. They were placed in the front line. Later the javelin (pilum) replaced the spear. The 'principes', from the Latin 'princeps' (chief), were so called because they had originally formed the front line. They were men in the prime of life, and now occupied the second line. Then came the 'triarii', tested veterans, who made up the third line, as their name indicated.

1 p. 61, *4*.

ROMAN TACTICS
1, a consular army. a, the first Roman legion with ten maniples of 'hastati' in the front line, the 'principes' in the second and the 'tirarii' in the third. b, the second legion. c, the cavalry consisting of right and left wings and reserve. d, the first and second allied legions. 2, 3, Vegetius in his work on military tactics distinguishes seven different orders of battle. The second and sixth are shown here. 2a, is initial position: a, heavy infantry; b, light infantry; c, cavalry and d, reserves. Green arrows show the enemy attack. 2b, a tactic where the left wing of the heavy infantry stands fast while the light infantry and cavalry attack from the rear. Meanwhile the right wing of heavy infantry executes a wheel. The reserve supports the left wing or gives cover to the right. 3a, initial position as before. The attacking enemy are the green arrows. 3b, a manoeuvre. The right wing assaults the enemy left flank while the left stands fast at an angle of 45 degrees, which directs the whole attack at the enemy left flank. 4, 5, 6, Roman standards. 7, silver eagle. 8, Roman eagle in heavily gilt bronze.

1

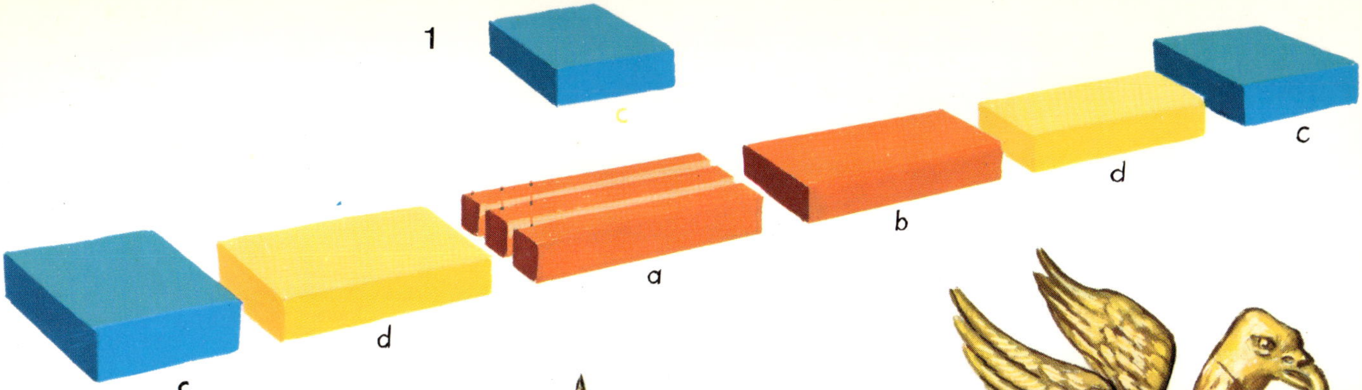

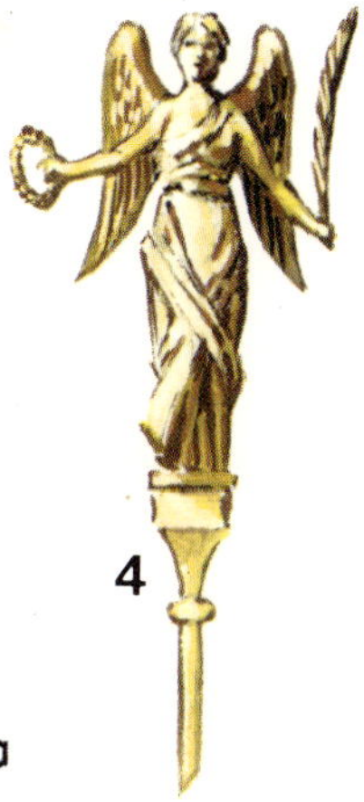

4

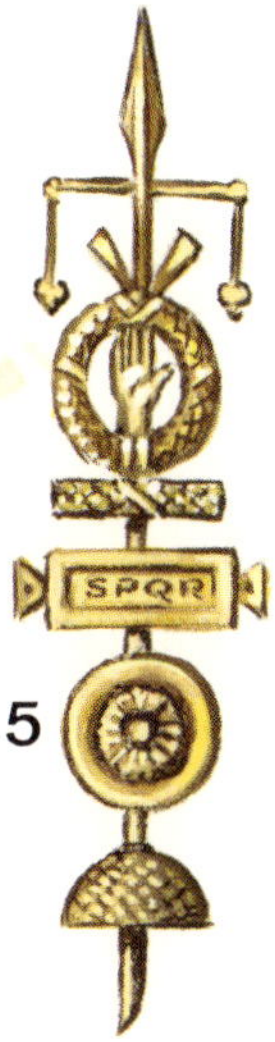

5

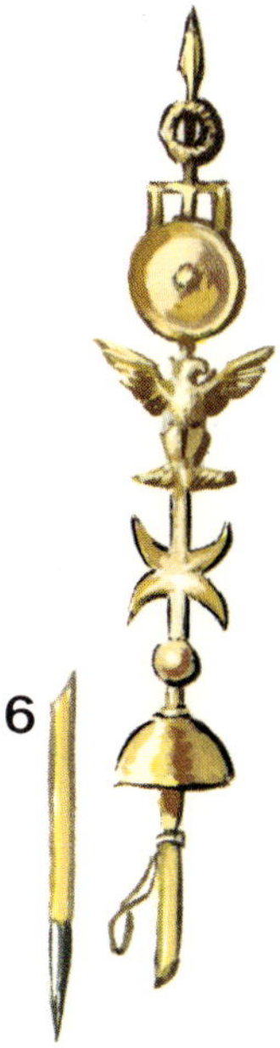

6

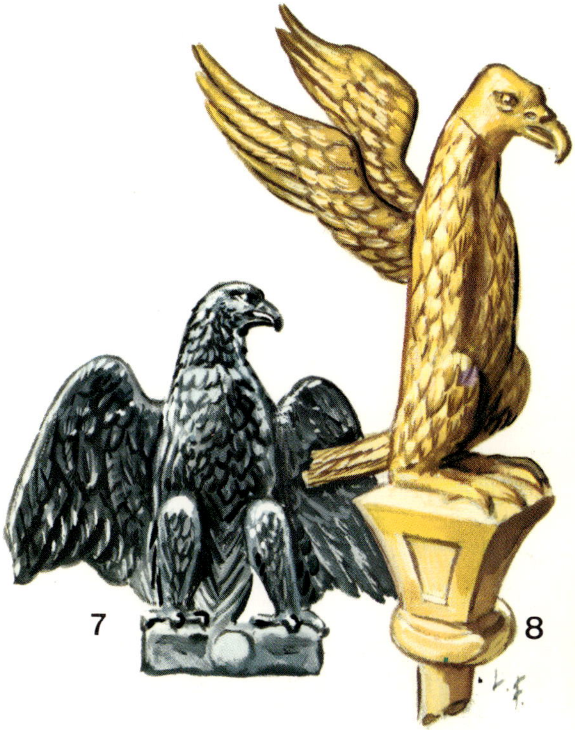

7

8

a

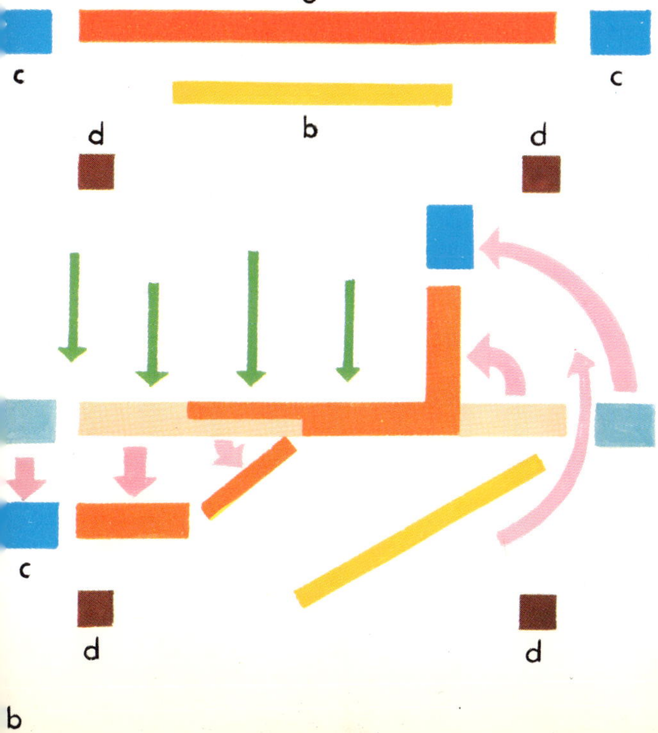

3a

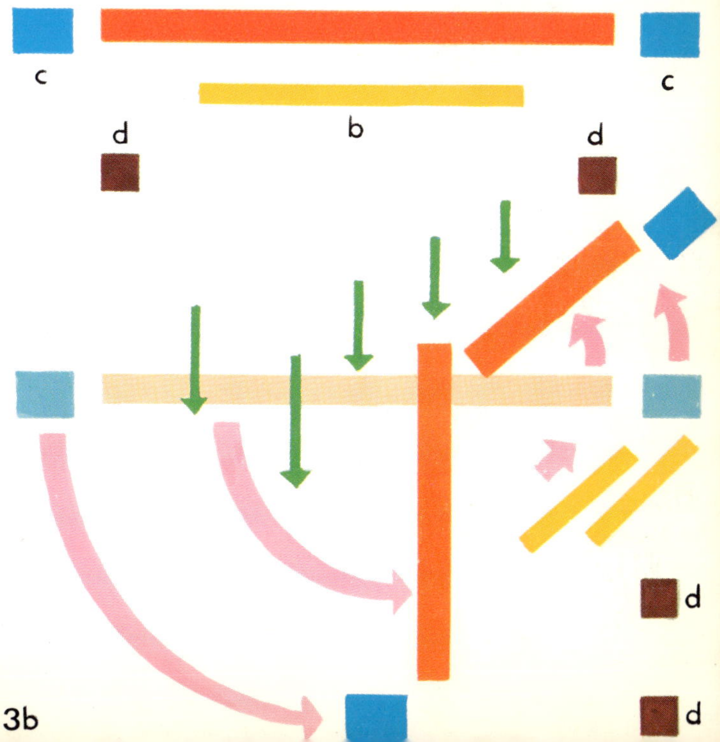

b

3b

The legion was divided into maniples, each of two centuries commanded by centurions. The senior centurion, the 'prior', commanded the maniple. The maniple developed into a tactical unit and for several centuries remained the base of the Roman legion.

Abandoning the principle of class distinction, the consul Marius made a radical reform, opening the ranks of the legion to every citizen, even the poorest. He gave Rome a massive army of well-trained professional soldiers trained for prolonged warfare.

The legion now numbered 6,000 men and its only emblem was the silver eagle,[1] which helped to develop loyalty and patriotism among the soldiers. The golden eagle[2] was not adopted until the time of the emperors. And so the history and traditions of the Roman legion began.

It was Marius also who evolved the 'cohort', a unit of 600 men, and one-tenth of a legion. Armament was standardized, and every soldier was equipped with the pilum.

Successor to Marius, Julius Caesar, gave each maniple its own standard, the standard of the central maniple being also the emblem of the legion.[3] The shields of each cohort were of different colours.

When he had subjugated Gaul, Caesar recruited into his army the best warriors from among the conquered. On the top of their helmets they wore a skylark and so were called the Alauda (skylark) legion.

Before Caesar's time, little attention was paid to the equipment of the auxiliaries who were lightly armed.

1, 2, 3, 4, soldiers of the Republic; 2 is a slinger. 5, 6, legionaries. 7, velite. 8, horseman. 9, legionary wearing segmented body armour. 10, sword. 11, parazonium and sword. 12, 13, helmets. 14, Greek-type sword. 15, dagger. 16, sword. 17, 18, helmets.

[1] p. 55, 7. [2] p. 55, 8. [3] p. 65, 5.

57

DEFENSIVE ARMS

The Roman soldier's defensive arms were the helmet, body armour, sword and leg-guards.

The helmet of leather (galea) of the earliest times was replaced by one of metal (cassis) under Camillus, only to reappear after the wars with Gaul. The cheek and chin-guards were often very large, as specimens found at Weisenau on the Rhine show. The helmets of Trajan's legionaries had a ring on the top so that they could be hung from the shoulder while on the march.[1]

The original body armour worn by the soldiers of Servius Tullius was of the Greek type. From the time of Marius, legionaries wore coats of mail, probably copied from the Gauls, called the 'lorica hamata'.[2] Another type, called the 'lorica squamata',[3] was reinforced with scales of iron, bone or bronze.

Later, at the end of the 1st Century AD, the body armour was improved. The 'lorica segmanta',[4] or jointed type, has been thought, but wrongly, to be the typically Roman form. The 'lorica segmanta' fell into disuse in the 3rd Century AD. This type of body armour was made of a corselet of circular iron bands hinged behind and fastening with a clasp over the chest, together with shoulder-pieces. It was worn over a brown woollen tunic.

Roman shields were basically of two types: the 'clipeus', or round shield, and the 'scutum',[5] or long shield which was oval or rectangular. At first, the clipeus seems more often to have been carried by the rich. Being made of bronze, it was too expensive for the poorer classes, who had to be content with a scutum of wood or wicker, oval or rectangular. The cavalry carried a round shield, smaller than the clipeus, called the 'parma'.

1, 2, standard-bearers. 3, officer. 4, centurion. 5, legionary. 6, 7, 8, leaden sling shot. Sometimes they bore the names of generals or towns and mottoes – even insults. 6, C. MARIUS, the famous Caius Marius who conquered the Cimbrians and Teutons (156–86 BC). 7, FERI CASSIUM ("Strike Cassius"), Cassius Longinus Varus was the Roman general who fought the bands of Spartacus (Consul in 73 BC). 8, ESUREIS ET ME CELAS ("You die of hunger and hide it from me"). Octavius (the future Augustus) at the siege of Perugia.

1 p. 57, *12–13/17–18*. 2 p. 61, *4/7*. 3 p. 61, *5/9*.
4 p. 63; p. 69, *1*. 5 p. 65, *4*.

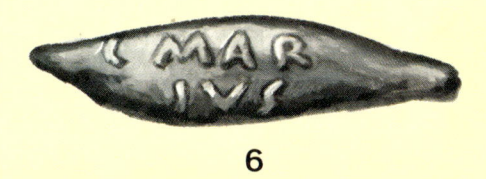

1 2 3 4 5

6 MARIVS

7 FERI CASSIVM

8 ESVREIS ET ME CELAS

59

From the 5th Century BC, the infantry adopted the light and inexpensive 'scutum'. It was oval and made of leather reinforced with a metal rim. According to Polybius, it measured 120 by 75 cm/ 47 by 29½ ins. For reasons of economy, towards the end of the 4th Century, the cavalry adopted the leather or wooden scutum.

Towards the time of Julius Caesar, the oval scutum was replaced by a rectangular shield, of curved cross-section.[1] It measured 120 by 80 cm/47 by 31½ ins and was made of two wooden panels so arranged that the grain of the wood ran in opposite ways. The outside was covered with leather and strengthened with a metal border. In the middle, on the boss or 'umbo',[2] were engraved the name and unit of the shield bearer. The rest of the shield was decorated with various motifs, called 'episemes'. The thunderbolt was often represented especially on the shields of the soldiers serving in the 'Lightning Legion'. These symbols were thought to give protection against evil.[3] The shield was supported on two leather thongs.

At the beginning of the Empire, there appeared a flat, hexagonal scutum of Celtic origin.[4] All these forms were later abandoned in favour of the ancient oval scutum (80 cms/34 ins across), but this too eventually gave way to the round shield and to that used by the Barbarians.

The final piece of defensive equipment was the greave, which from the time of Servius was worn by the two upper classes. Under Marius, its use was limited to the officers.

The Roman soldiers wore a sandal, with bronze nails, called the 'calego', which extended a short way up the leg.[5]

1, foot-soldier wearing the 'sagum'. 2, 3, light infantry 'buccinatores'. 4, hastatus. 5, cavalry musician. 6, officer wearing a 'paludamentum'. 7, legionary wearing coat of mail and scarf (focale). 8, legionary 'buccinator'. 9, centurion. 10, slinger, German auxiliary. 1, 3, 4, 5, 6, 7, 8, 9, are wearing breeches copied from the Gauls. 11, Roman sword. 12, sword of the classical period. 13, 14, swords and scabbards. 15, 16, 'pilum'. 17, quiver. 18, officer's sword. 19, Iberian sword. 20, sling. 4 and 7 are wearing the coat of mail called 'lorica hamata'. 5 and 9 the body armour reinforced with scales, 'lorica squamata'.

---

1 p. 57, *9*; p. 69, *1*.   2 From *umbilicus* meaning navel.
3 They were supposed to protect one against ill-omens and evil spirits.   4 p. 57, *8*; p. 59, *5*; p. 65, *4*.
5 p. 69, *2/3*.

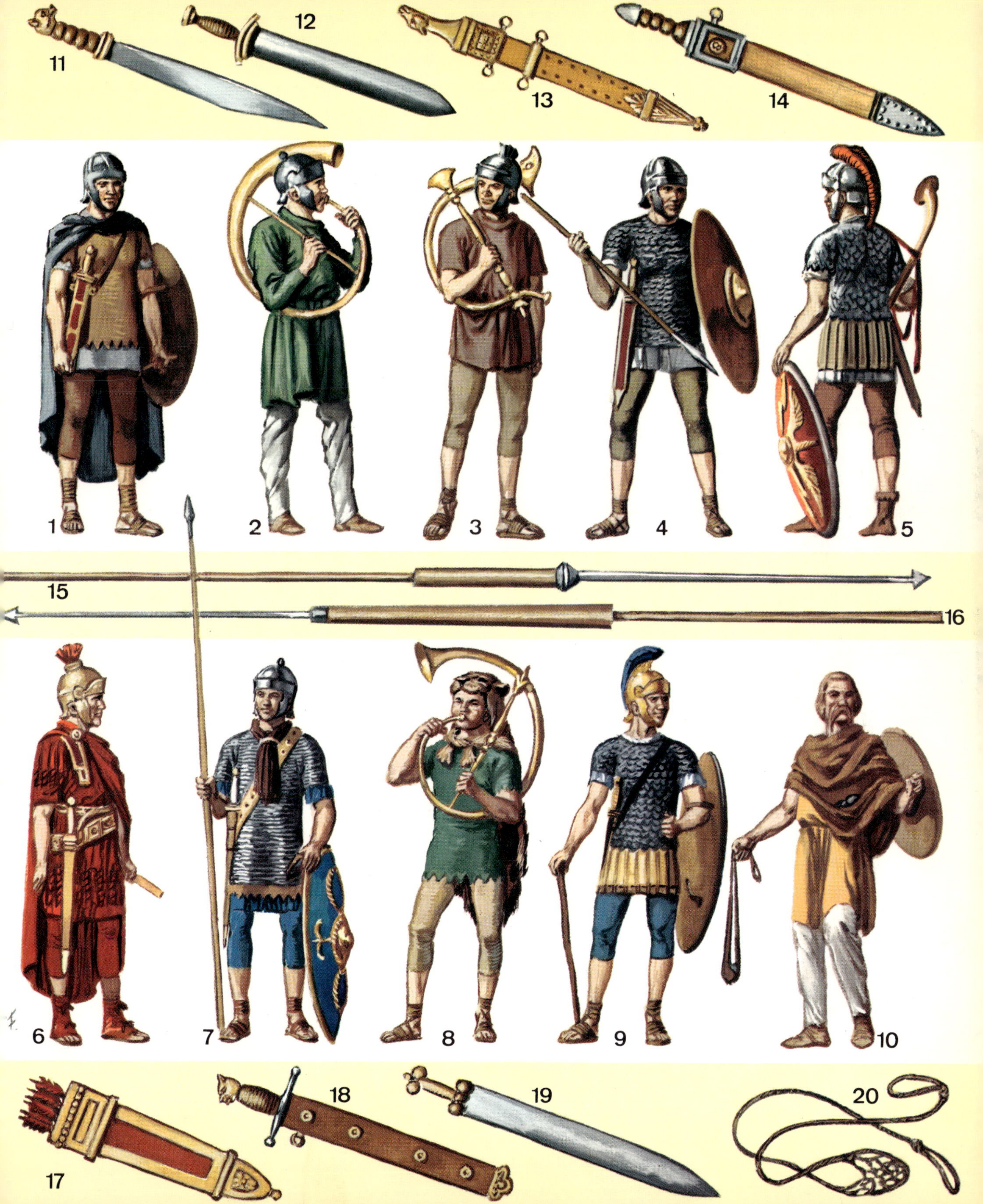
11
12
13
14
1
2
3
4
5
15
16
6
7
8
9
10
17
18
19
20

OFFENSIVE WEAPONS

Originally, the Romans used a sword of the Greek type.[1] Following the example of Hannibal, however, they adopted a longer and heavier weapon, the Iberian sword,[2] the Spanish swordsmiths being at that time the finest in the world. The sword was carried on the right thigh in a scabbard of wood covered with leather.[3] The hilt had a long pommel and the grip was shaped to the hand. The blade, originally 50 cms/20 ins long, was increased to 80 cms/31½ ins during the reign of Augustus.

In the 3rd Century AD, there appeared the 'spartha', until then used only by the auxiliaries. This weapon was nearly 1 m/3 ft long, including the hilt. This lengthening of the sword marks the decline of the Roman Empire, which, with more and more mercenaries, turned away from the hand-to-hand fighting of the earlier centuries, no longer having the nerve and skill demanded by this form of combat.

Much more important than the sword was the javelin. The origins of the 'pilum', which Montesquieu describes as having conquered the Universe, are uncertain. It differed from the spear in the length of the head[4] which made up at least a third of its overall length of some 2 m/6½ ft. In early times, each soldier carried two pila of different weights. The lighter one weighed 2 kg/4¼ lbs, the heavier 2½ kg/5 lbs. Both had heavy shafts.

Marius made an important modification to the pilum. The blade was now secured to the shaft by two pins, one of iron and the other of wood. When the spear struck a shield, the weaker wooden pin sheered and the shaft, pivoting on the iron pin, dragged along the ground. The legionary could then put his foot on it, causing the

THE DEFEAT OF THE CIMBRIANS

A triumph of strategy and discipline, the victory of Marius over the Cimbrians (101 BC) near Vercelli, in Piedmont, saved the Roman civilization.

---

1 p. 57, *14*.   2 p. 61, *19*.   3 p. 57, *16*; p. 61, *13/14/18*.   4 p. 61, *15/16*.

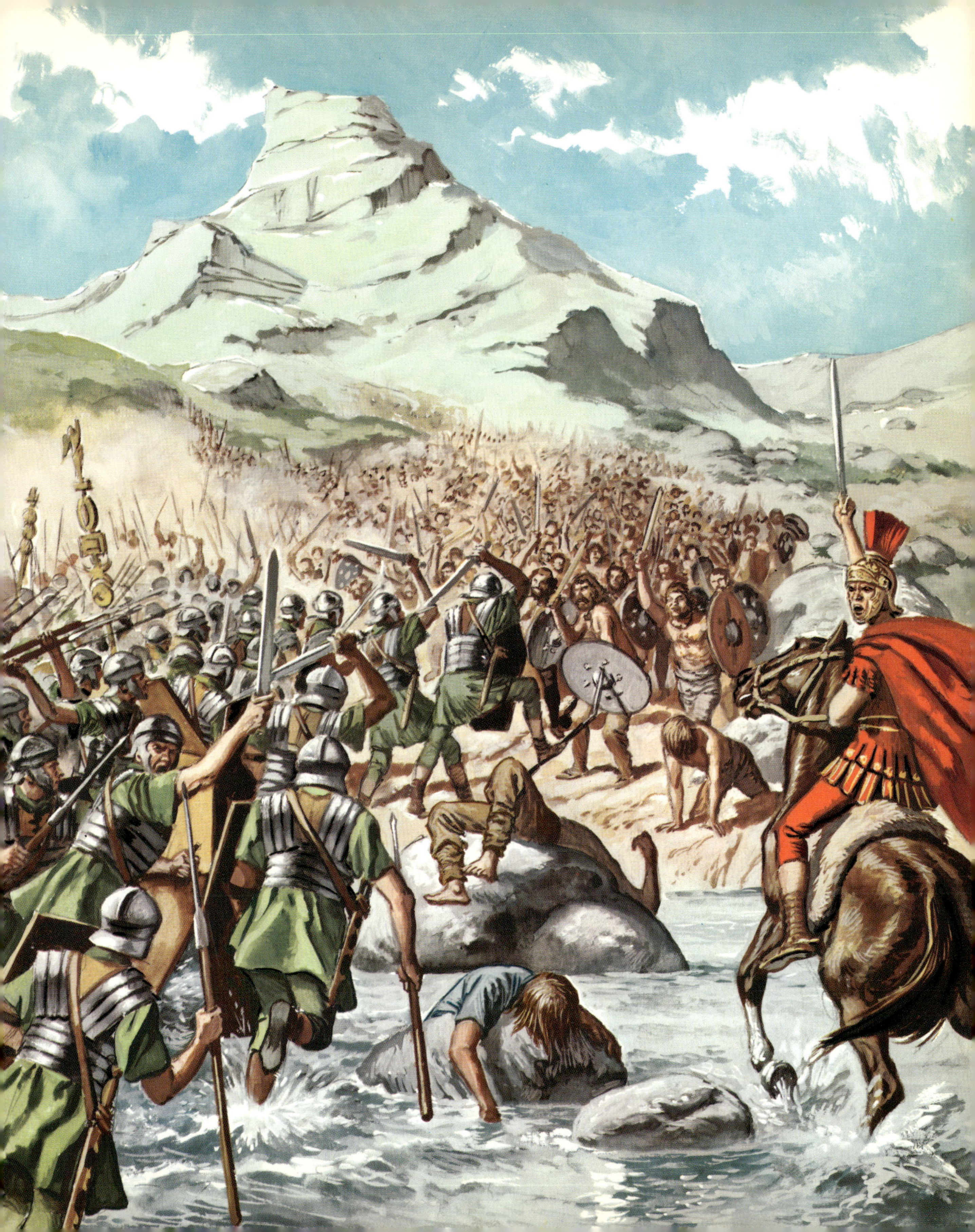

enemy shield to drop and expose his adversary to the sword.[1] According to the weight, the range of the pilum varied from 20–40 m/68–136 ft. Experiments have shown that the pilum could pierce a piece of wood 3 cms/1¼ ins thick. The heavy pilum was used more in close combat.

The Roman cavalry, originally a force of 300 horsemen, increased to 1,800 under Servius Tullius. Foreign wars soon necessitated still further expansion.

After the Second Punic War, the Romans recruited large numbers of auxiliaries from amongst the conquered peoples and these replaced the regular cavalry.

The dress of the cavalry was very much like that of the infantry. The horse had a leather or cloth blanket held by a girth but without saddle or stirrups. A bridle, bit (but no curb), head-stall and reins completed the harness. The Romans did use 'hipposandals', but it has been shown from the discovery of a skeleton of a horse in Germany that they also practised shoeing.

The cavalry was composed of archers, 'equites sagitarii', and spearmen, 'contarii', usually Gauls. Germans, Sarmatians and Numidians. The Sarmatians provided heavy cavalry, called 'cataphractus'. The cataphraetaries[2] had a role similar to that of the men-at-arms in Europe at the beginning of the 14th Century.

ROMAN CAVALRY

1, 3, Roman horsemen. 2, Barbarian 'cataphractus'. 4, horseman with leather cuirass. 5, standard-bearer (vexillum) of the time of Constantine.

---

[1] The picture on p. 63 shows a soldier using the pilum. [2] p. 65, *2*.

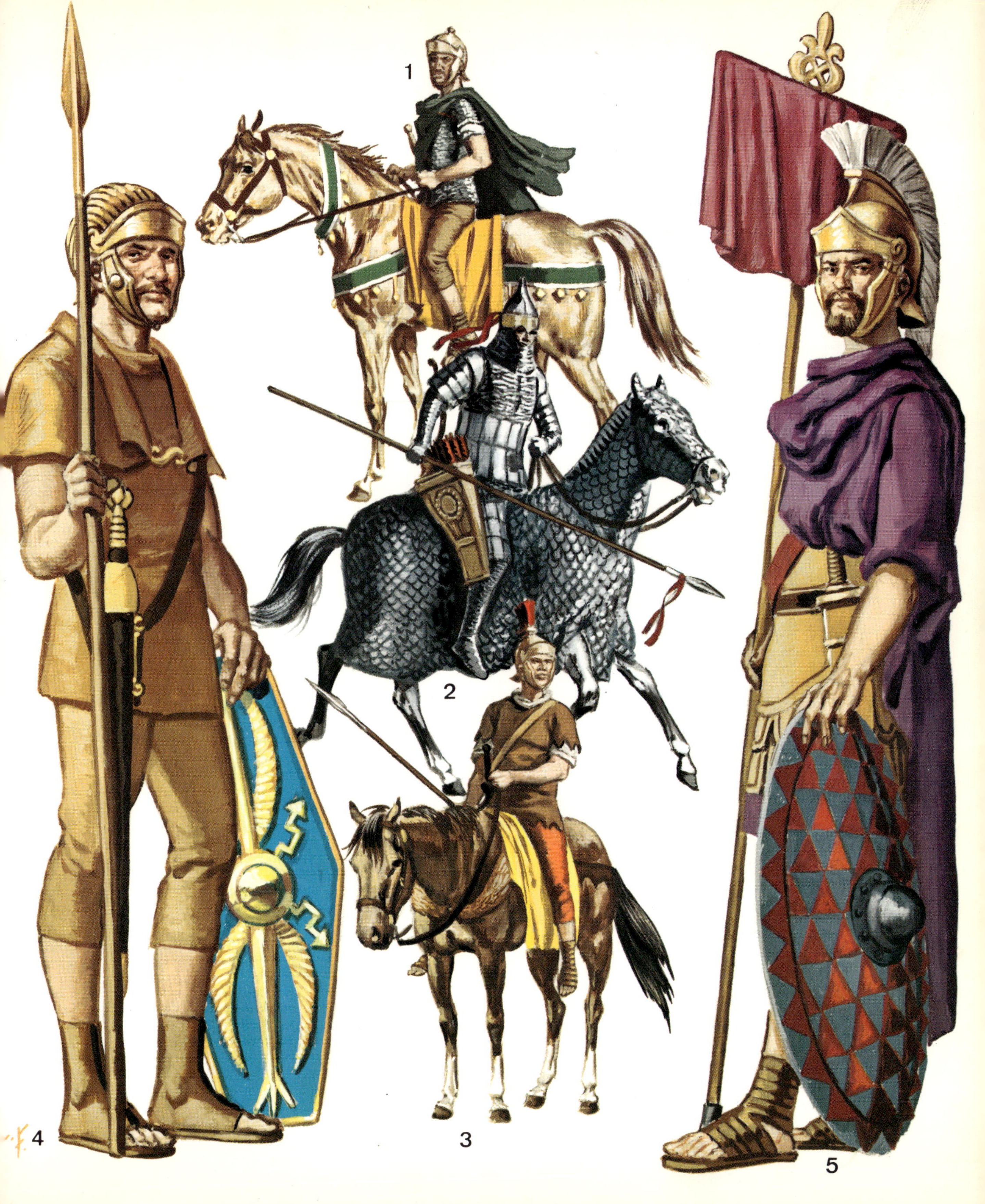
1
2
3
4
5

WAR MACHINES

Very early on, the Romans developed a large range of war machines designed for defending towns.

At the time of the Empire, the train of the legion included 55 wheeled 'ballistae' drawn by teams of mules. The missiles from the ballista could pierce the thickest body armour. Ten 'onagers', or 'scorpions' drawn by oxen completed the artillery. The use of these machines became widespread under Hadrian.

Other war machines included battering-rams of various sizes, called 'ambulatores', mobile towers and siege ballistae and catapults that could throw missiles weighing over 30 kg/66 lbs.

There were also mobile 'mantlets', the 'tortoise', a covered gallery giving protection to the sappers, the 'tollenon', a beam that hoisted a basket loaded with soldiers onto the walls and, lastly, a form of grapnel designed to tear down the enemy's ramparts.

As we have mentioned in the chapter on the Greeks, the Romans employed war-elephants. These elephants had iron plates protecting the head, flanks, chest, trunk and tusks. On the back, they carried a turret manned by archers and javelin throwers. The elephant spreads its ears when angry, so these were painted in vivid colours to make the animals even more terrifying. To make it more aggressive, the animal was made drunk on an aromatic wine, which occasionally made it more of a problem to its own side than to the enemy's! However, as a rule, elephants were little used and they disappeared completely at the time of Hadrian.

The legion had its own military music, played by 'tubicines' (tuba-players), 'buccinatores', 'cornicines', whose instrument (cornu) was less curved than the 'buccina', and the 'liticines', who played the piercing 'lituus'.[1]

1 p. 61, *2/3/5/8*.

WAR MACHINES

1, onager or scorpion. 2, ballista which could hurl a missile up to 400 ms/1,300 ft. 3, battering-ram. 4, catapult capable of throwing missiles weighing up to 100 kg/ 220 lbs.

67

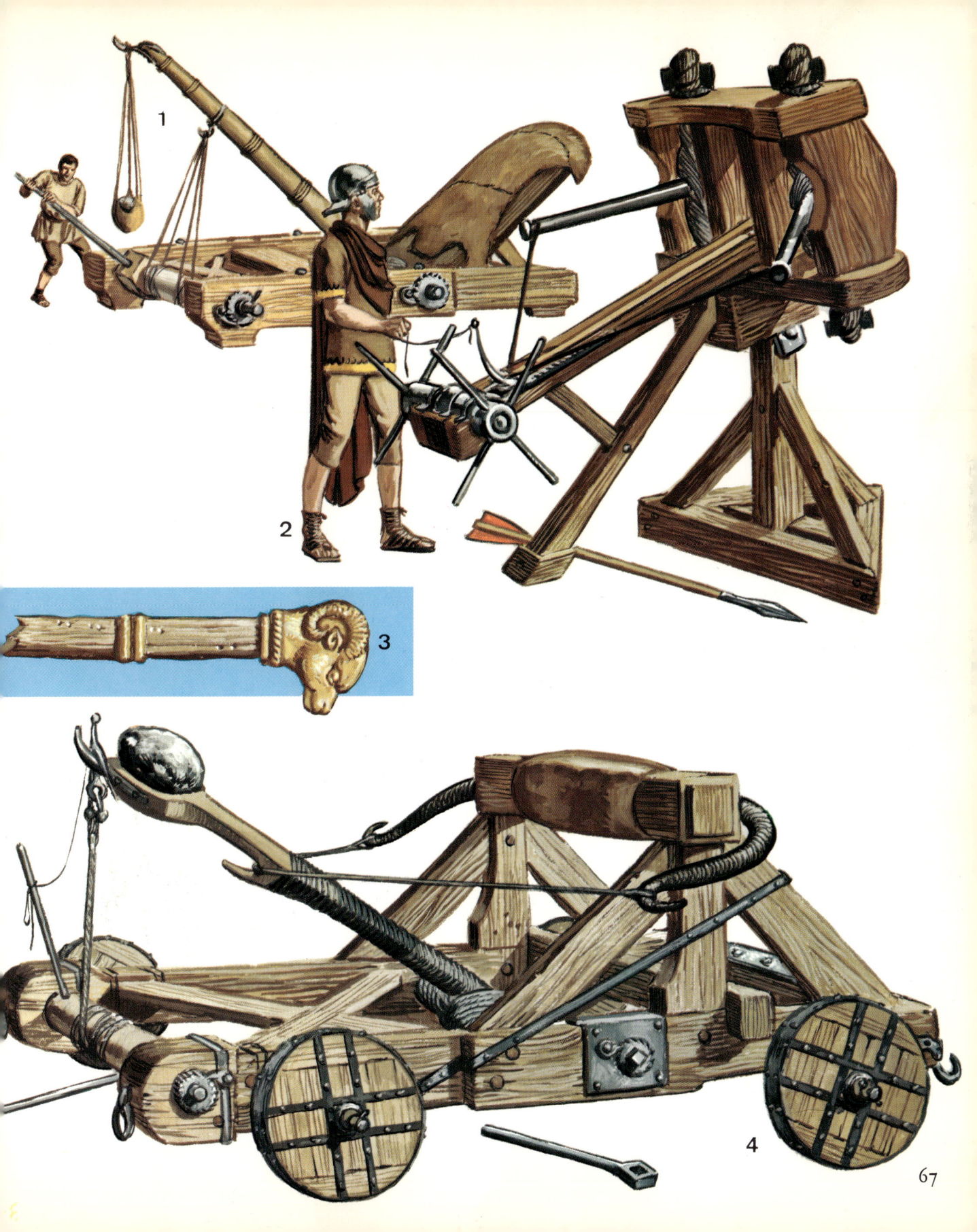

The Roman soldier carried everything he needed on his back, a weight of about 60 Roman pounds (a Roman pound was equivalent to 327·5 grms/12 oz). So he was well loaded, what with his weapons, bedding, spade, axe, basket and cooking utensils, not to mention a fortnight's ration of flour.[1] At each halt he had to build a camp, which involved digging trenches and constructing ramparts,[2] even if it was to be only for one day.

The soldier left his baggage in the camp when he marched out to fight. Unencumbered, he was then named 'expeditus' – ready for battle.

1, fully loaded (impeditus) legionary. 2, ordinary soldier's footwear. 3, officer's footwear. 4, frying pan with handle. 5, camp: A, Praetorian gate; B, Decanian gate; C, main gate; D, Quinton gate; E, general's tent; F, officers' tent behind which are the legions' various standards; G, legionaries' tents; G¹, auxiliaries' tents; H, guard houses (stationes). 6, cross-section of Roman camp: a, ditch; b, palisade; c, parapet; d, access ramp.

[1] p. 69, *1*. [2] p. 69, *5/6*

69

Gladiators

There was a popular song in the amphitheatres that ran: "*Non te peto, piscem peto; quid me fugis, Galle?* (I'm not after you, I'm after the fish; why do you flee from me, Gaul?)"

The Gaulish gladiator who appeared in the bloody games of the arena in the time of Caesar, wore a helmet ornamented with a fish. Under the empire, he was to become the famous traditional opponent or the retiary.

Originally, gladiatorial combats had a religious significance, for they were human sacrifices made to some illustrious personage no longer living, but later the people acquired a taste for these bloodthirsty proceedings and they developed into public spectacles that enjoyed an extraordinary popularity under the Empire.

The Romans classified the gladiators by their weapons, by their method of fighting, and often by the name of their country of origin. The oldest type was the 'Samnite', a category that later was divided into the 'secutor' and the 'oplomachus'. The 'Thracian' appeared in the time of Sylla, and the 'retiary' with Julius Caesar. The retiary, armed only with a net and trident, was the lowliest of all.

The gladiators were given additional titles according to other circumstances. They were called 'meridiani' if they fought at noon, 'supposititii' when they replaced the wounded or vanquished and 'postulatitii' when they were specially acclaimed by the crowd.

Ancient authors mention other categories about which we have little reliable information – the 'equites', gladiators on horseback, the 'essedarius', who fought from a chariot, the 'andabate', who fought blindfold and the 'laquearius', armed with a rope.

Public notices announced the gladiatorial combats. Here is one taken from a wall at Pompeii:

"The troupe of gladiators of Numerius Festus Ampliatus will make a second appearance on the 16th day of the June Kalends."

The spectacle began with a parade led by the 'editor', organizer of the festivities; then the gladiators took part in mock fights with the staff (rudis) with wooden or iron weapons (arma lusoria). Finally, the trumpets would announce the beginning of the fighting in earnest. As soon as a gladiator was wounded the crowd would cry out: "*Hoc habet!*" ('He's had it!') The wounded man would lift his left hand to ask for mercy. If he had fought bravely the crowd would spare his life by giving the thumbs-up sign; if not, they would turn their thumbs downwards, signifying that the man must die. The unexpected arrival of the Emperor in the middle of a fight would automatically spare the lives of the wounded. Sometimes the same prerogative was extended to the vestal virgins and the editor.

The Roman people delighted in these bloody sports, without raising feelings of horror. Even Cicero considered dying gladiators as models of steadfastness and courage.

The gladiators' helmets had an interesting feature, they were fitted with a visor that completely masked the face. Perhaps the Romans had already hit on the idea exploited by the organizers of modern wrestling, that the mystery of the identity of the 'Masked Man' pulls in the crowds in their hundreds. But even if the public do flock to such modern-day gladiatorial displays, happily half of them do so only to laugh at these parodies of the fight to the death.

GLADIATORS
1, veles. 2, retiary. 3, 4, mounted gladiators. 5, mirmillion. 6, secutor. *Left* and *right*, gladiators' helmets with movable visors.

71

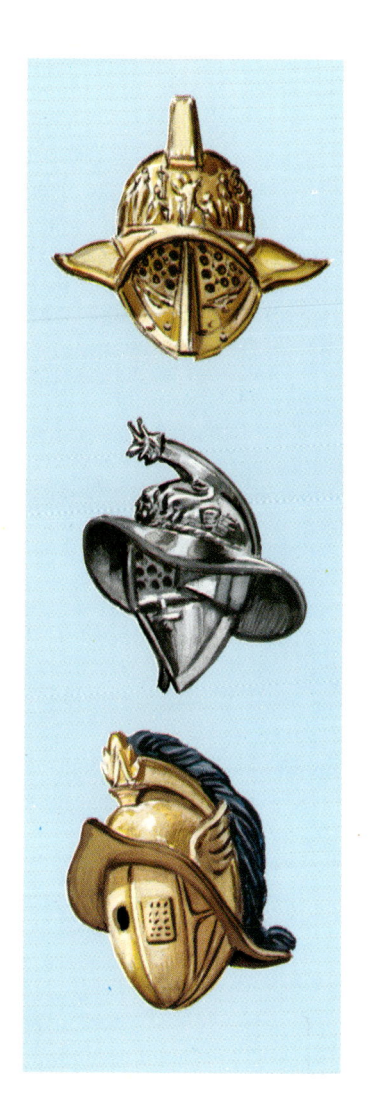

The Gauls

From birth, the young Gaul was brought up to become a valiant warrior. Scantily clad, forced to swim in icy waters, he was trained in the use of arms up to the age of fifteen, when he received from his father a sword and shield he must not lay down until death.

The young warrior then joined a warlike band under the leadership of a veteran chief whose prowess he admired. Several of these bands combined together to form a circle with greater or lesser ambitions; spurred on by ambition and competition, the Gauls then reached to the height of their power.

In 400 BC, they marched on Latium after invading the Rhone Valley. In 390 BC, they marched on Rome and routed the hastily assembled defenders, thanks to a cunning move on the part of their chief, Brennus. The Romans had to pay 1,000 lbs/453·6 kg of gold to the conquerors.

For six generations the Gauls extended their conquests, reaching Corinth in 368 BC. It needed the reputation of Alexander to keep them in check but, after the death of that great general, they became active again, over-running Greece and the Balkans. These tall, blond, blue-eyed men were absolutely indifferent to death and accomplished the most heroic feats of arms.

In the first Gaulish armies, the infantry made up a considerable part. Brennus mustered 150,000 foot-soldiers before Rome as against only 20,000 cavalry – though the horsemen were the pick of his army.

The Gauls fought bare-chested. They wore trousers gathered at the ankle, the 'sagum' (a woollen cloak) attached to the shoulder with a clasp. The sagum was later adopted by the Romans as the military cloak.[1]

1, ancient British hill fortification. 2, Gaulish stronghold: a, outer wall and towers; b, fortified entrance; c, vegetable garden; d, living quarters. The floors of the long low huts were sunk into the ground to a depth of about 1 m/3 ft; e, inner precinct with ditch and stronghold (forerunner of moat and bailey). 3, cross-section of outer wall showing beams incorporated to give added strength against siege-engines.

[1] p. 75.

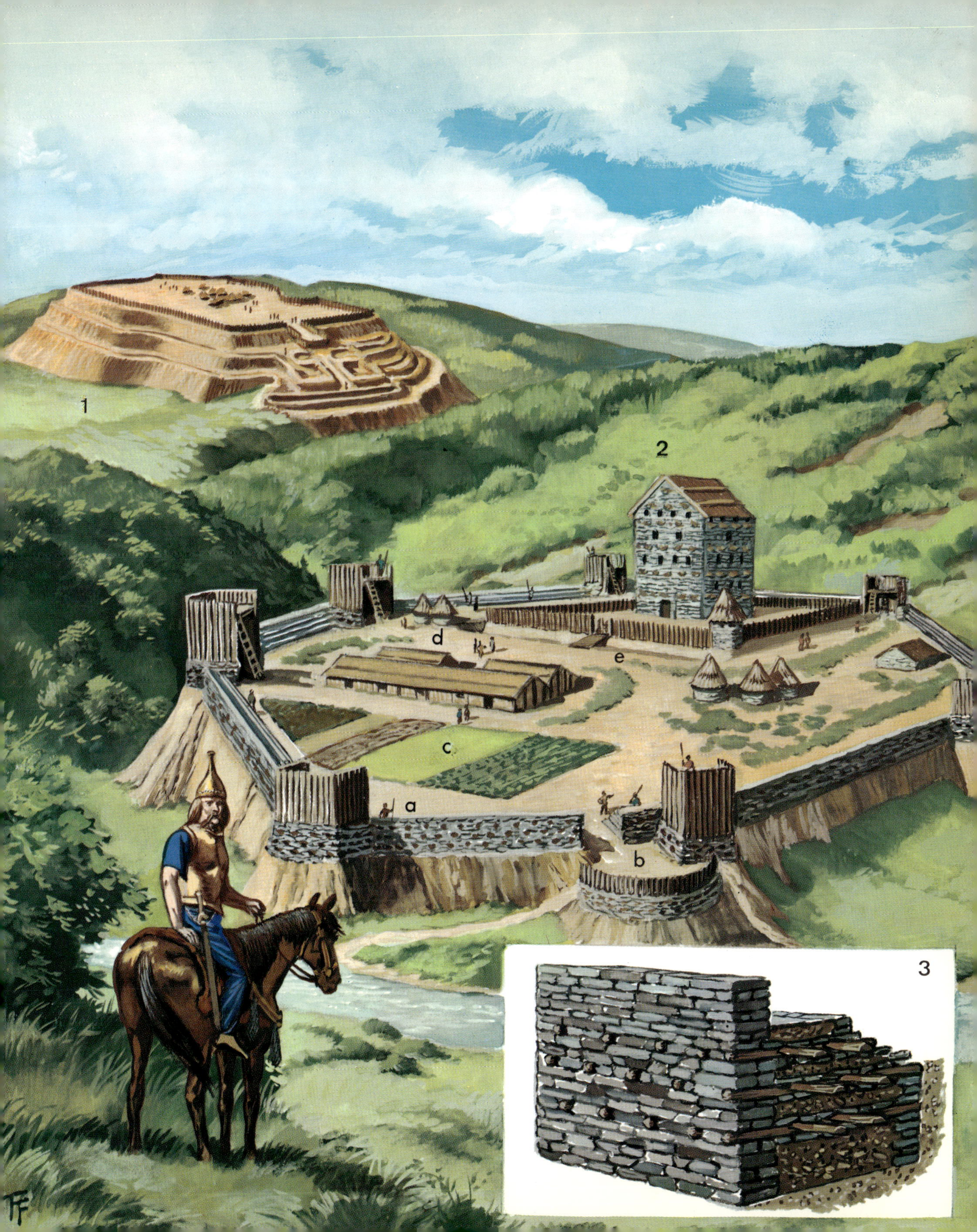
1
2
d
e
c
a
b
3

The Gaul made little use of defensive equipment; his shield, a poorly made and clumsy affair, was of woven wicker covered with leather, or of thick strips of wood joined together and covered with skin.[1] Sometimes a shield would have the head of some animal nailed to it as an ornament; the more well-to-do would show patterns or masks embossed in bronze on their shields.

The Gauls' helmets were of bronze or iron,[2] and decorated with various fanciful objects. Some bore horns, birds' wings, or boars' heads and the heads of other animals in bold relief, but these were worn only by the chiefs.

Breastplates, which were not much used, were of bronze or iron made like the Greek models.[3] There were two other types of body-armour: one of chain-mail[4] and the other of several thicknesses of material glued together like those of the Egyptians.

1, 2, 3, Gaulish warriors. 4, British warrior. 5, 6, 7, Gaulish warriors. 8, British chief. 9, Gaul with 'carnix' (trumpet). 10, Gaul wearing coat of mail. 11, 12, 13, 14, helmets of iron and bronze. 15, 16, bronze breastplates. 17, Celtic axe. 18, 19, iron and bronze daggers. 20, axe. 21, iron sword.

OFFENSIVE WEAPONS

Above all other weapons the Gaul favoured the long iron sword,[5] over 1 m/3 ft in length and 4–5 cms/1½–2 ins broad, which he used with a chopping motion.[6] Being badly tempered, it buckled after the first few strokes, and its poor quality was one of the causes of the defeats inflicted on the Gauls by Rome. It was worn at the right side on an iron or bronze chain.

The Gauls kept huge reserves of this weapon, so much so that Hannibal was able to equip his entire army with it from stocks taken from the Allobroges alone.

As a throwing weapon the Gauls had only a kind of pike-javelin

[1] p. 77, *10*. [2] p. 75. [3] p. 75, *15/16*. [4] p. 75, *10*.
[5] p. 75, *21*; p. 77, *1/2/3/4*. [6] With the point.

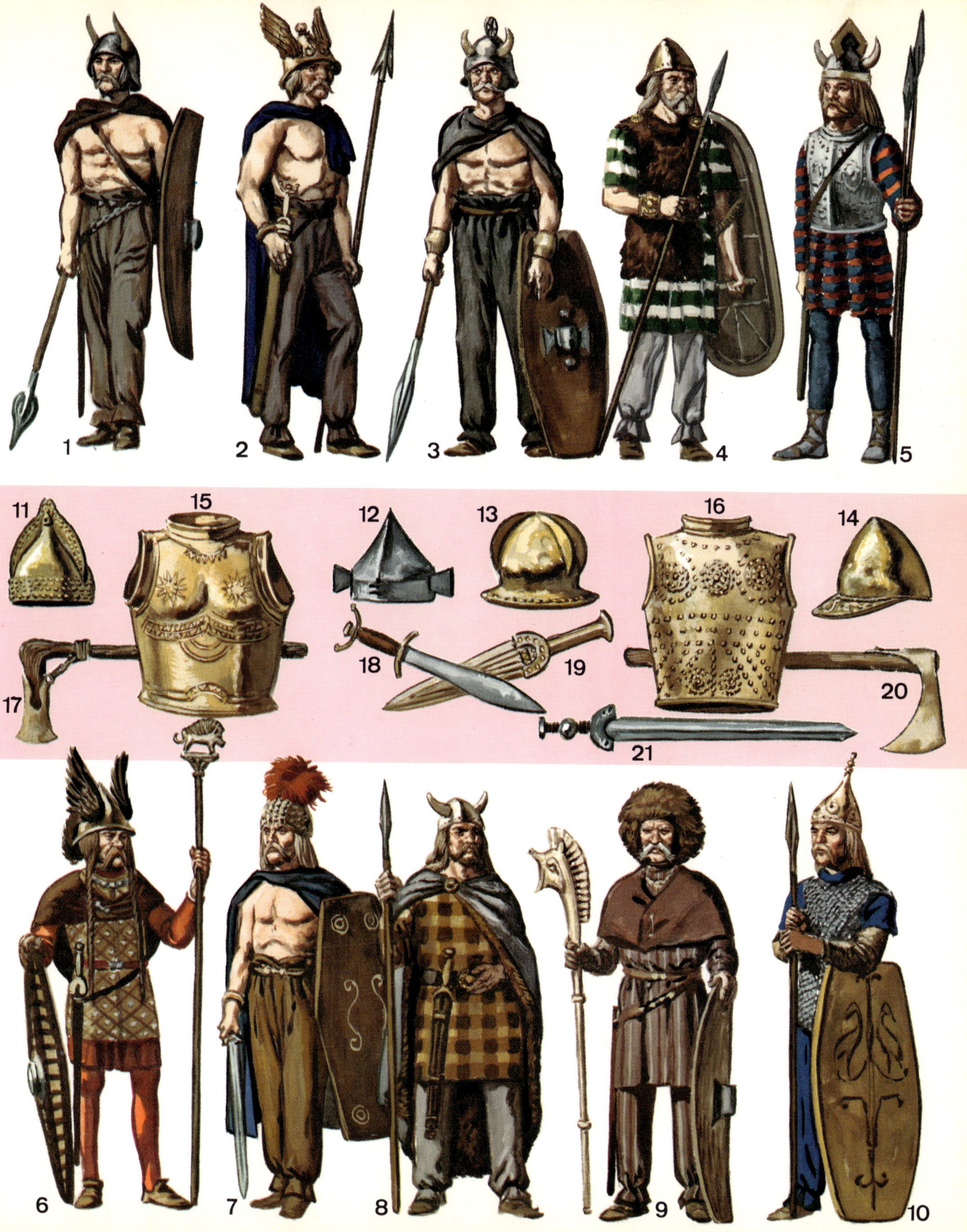
1
2
3
4
5
11
15
12
13
16
14
17
18
19
20
21
6
7
8
9
10

that was badly balanced and had a short range. Strabo calls them 'matares' and Diodorus of Sicily 'saunies'. The blade was up to 50 cms/20 ins long and was sometimes hooked at the tip.

The sling, with which the Gauls were familiar, was used mainly during sieges to hurl red-hot balls of clay that set fire to the tents and huts within the Roman fortifications.

The secondary armament consisted of the dagger, the axe and the mace. The mace was carried mostly by the cavalry, hanging from the saddle bow.

1, 2, 3, 4, sword-hilts. 2 is the earliest. 5, 6, 7, 8, 9, iron and bronze spear-heads. 10, inside of shield. 11, 12, bronze axe-heads. 13, carnix. 14, 15, standards in form of boar and cock. 16, Gaulish warrior and chariot.

TACTICS

The Gauls used much the same tactics as the Barbarians. Their foot-soldiers attacked in close order behind the shelter of their shields. In the front rank were the picked men, distinguished by gold rings round their arms and necks.

Disdainful of subterfuge and full of a naive pride that made them eager to engage in hand-to-hand combat, the Gauls charged at the sound of the 'carnix', shouting and grimacing at the enemy, crowded round their standards which were usually in the form of a bronze boar, their symbol of strength and power.[1]

The cavalry manoeuvres were likewise simple; they charged flat out brandishing their swords, happy that thus they would paralyse the enemy with fright.

Chariots were used almost exclusively by the tribes of the Belgae, who handled them with great skill. Drawn-up together these

1 p. 77, *14*.

77

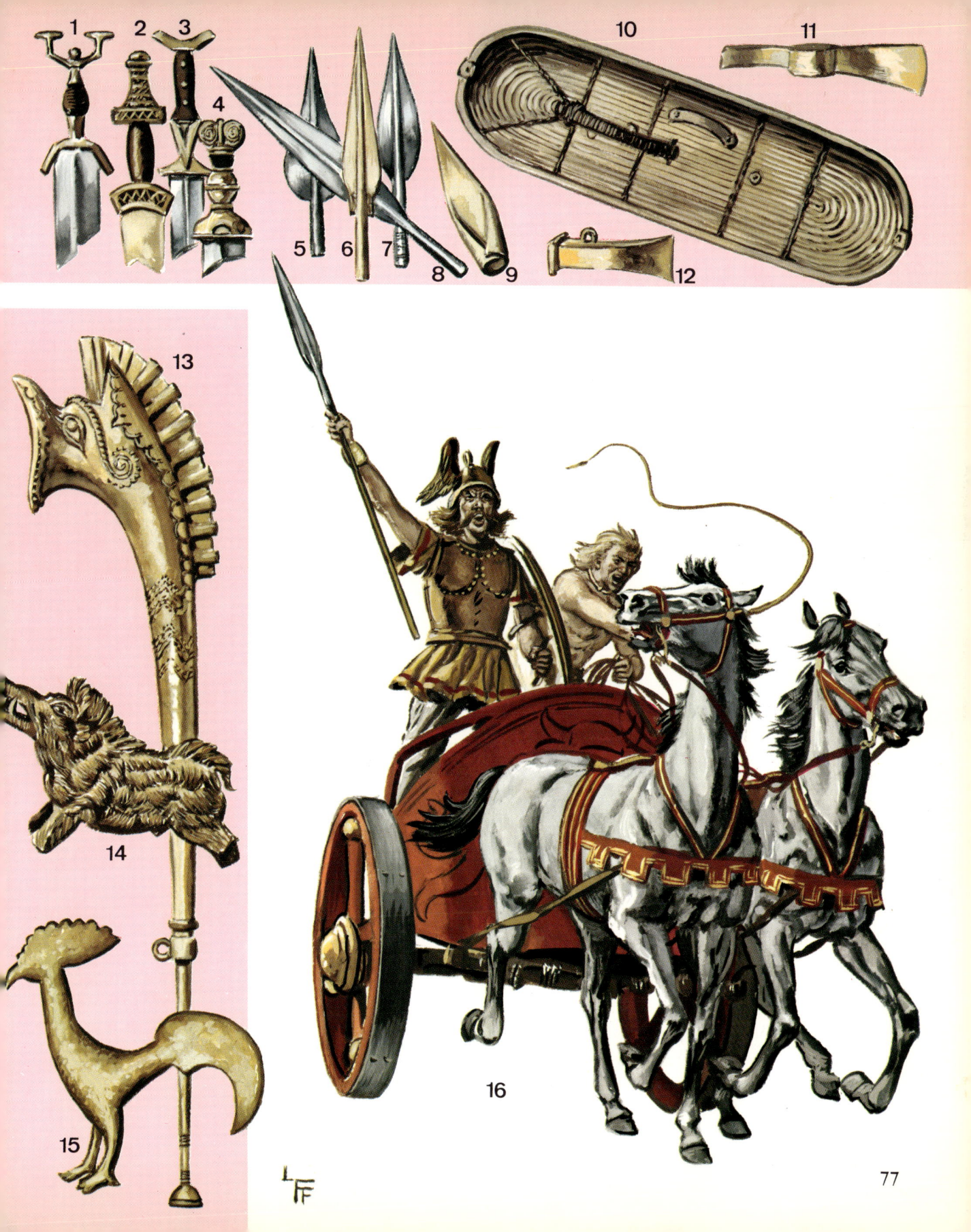

chariots made an effective line of defence. They had each a crew of two soldiers.[1]

Fearless of death, and considering it a privilege to fall weapon in hand, the Gauls knew no pity, but sacrificed to their god Teutates, the corpses of the vanquished, and proudly exhibited their heads hanging from their horses' necks.

FORTIFICATIONS

Although little advance had been made with regard to weapons, great strides had been made in the protection of cities. The Gauls rebuilt and strengthened the defences of the towns that they had taken. The 'oppidum' appeared, a fortress designed specifically to withstand battering-rams and the other war-machines used in siege warfare by the Romans.[2]

Julius Caesar in his *Commentaries* records his distaste for such fortresses and the waste of time and the rebuffs they caused him. He had to destroy 800 of them before he had conquered Gaul.

Everyone should read and re-read that great writer. As Montaigne, timeless student of the *Commentaries*, says "Only God knows with what grace and beauty he has vested that priceless story, so pure, so delicate, so perfect, that, for me, no other writing in the world can, in this respect, compare with it".

1, chariot of a tribe of Belgae living in Britain (about 150–100 BC the Belgae, who were related to the Gauls, crossed the English Channel and conquered the whole of Britain except the extreme north). 2, warrior of an ancient Scottish tribe. 3, Gaulish horseman. 4, Germano-Roman horseman. 5, Anglo-Roman soldier.

1 p. 77, *16*; p. 79, *1*.   2 p. 73.

1

2

3

4

5

The Great Invasions

Liou-ts'ong and his Huns had founded in China in the 4th Century, a short-lived empire doomed to destruction by hordes of Turks, Mongols and Tibetans. Pressed from the north by the Jouan-Jouan and from the south by the Tibetans, the Huns were driven west by the Yue-tche, the warlike Indo-Scythians.

The westward drive of the Huns was irresistible. They defeated the Alani and the Goths of the Russian plain, who, in their turn, retreated driving the Germans before them towards the Atlantic.

It was this shift of population that was to destroy the Roman empire in the West.

Like the Gauls, the Germans put the profession of arms above all others. Likely youngsters were given a sword with which they were first dubbed three times on the shoulder and, thereafter, they took their place in warlike expeditions. The infantry played the most important part. Cavalry were rare, though they were highly thought of.

After the fashion of the Gauls, the Germans, too, wore cloth cloaks, but also, at times, clad themselves in the skins of wild animals, the fur of which they dyed.

They were very proud of their long hair which they dyed red.

DEFENSIVE WEAPONS

The wearing of helmets was confined to the chiefs. The oblong shields served not only to protect the body but also as stretchers, as cover in open country, and as floats when swimming across rivers. Only seasoned warriors had the privilege of decorating their shields. The shields of young soldiers remained plain until they had taken part in some famous feat of arms and their courage had been proved. Then they were allowed to display some suitable symbol. From this custom hereditary armorial bearings developed.[1]

OFFENSIVE WEAPONS

There were two kinds of sword; a short one, called a 'swerd', carried at the waist, and a long one not sharpened at the point, called a 'spad', 'spada' or 'spatha'.[2]

Another weapon much favoured by the Germans was the 'scramasax', a form of cutlass with a single edge.[3] Later came the battle-axe, often double-bladed, and a javelin, the 'framea'. The bow seems to have been little used in war.

TACTICS

Like the Gauls, the Germans used only primitive tactics, which seem to have been limited to deployment for defence in open country and to attacking in close column.

The German 'oppida' were like those of the Gauls.

The dense forests formed a natural and almost impenetrable system of defences. By hedging coppices and saplings, they built living entanglements through which no invader could pass.

1 p. 81, *1–2*.   2 p. 81, *10*.   3 p. 81, *9*.

THE BARBARIANS

1, 2, Germans; 2 is a new recruit. 3, Scot. The Scots invaded Caledonia (Scotland) which was the territory of the Picts. 4, Bavarian warrior. 5, German standard-bearer. 6, German. 7, Visigoth. 8, axe-head. 9, scramasax. 10, spatha. 11, double-edged axe-head.

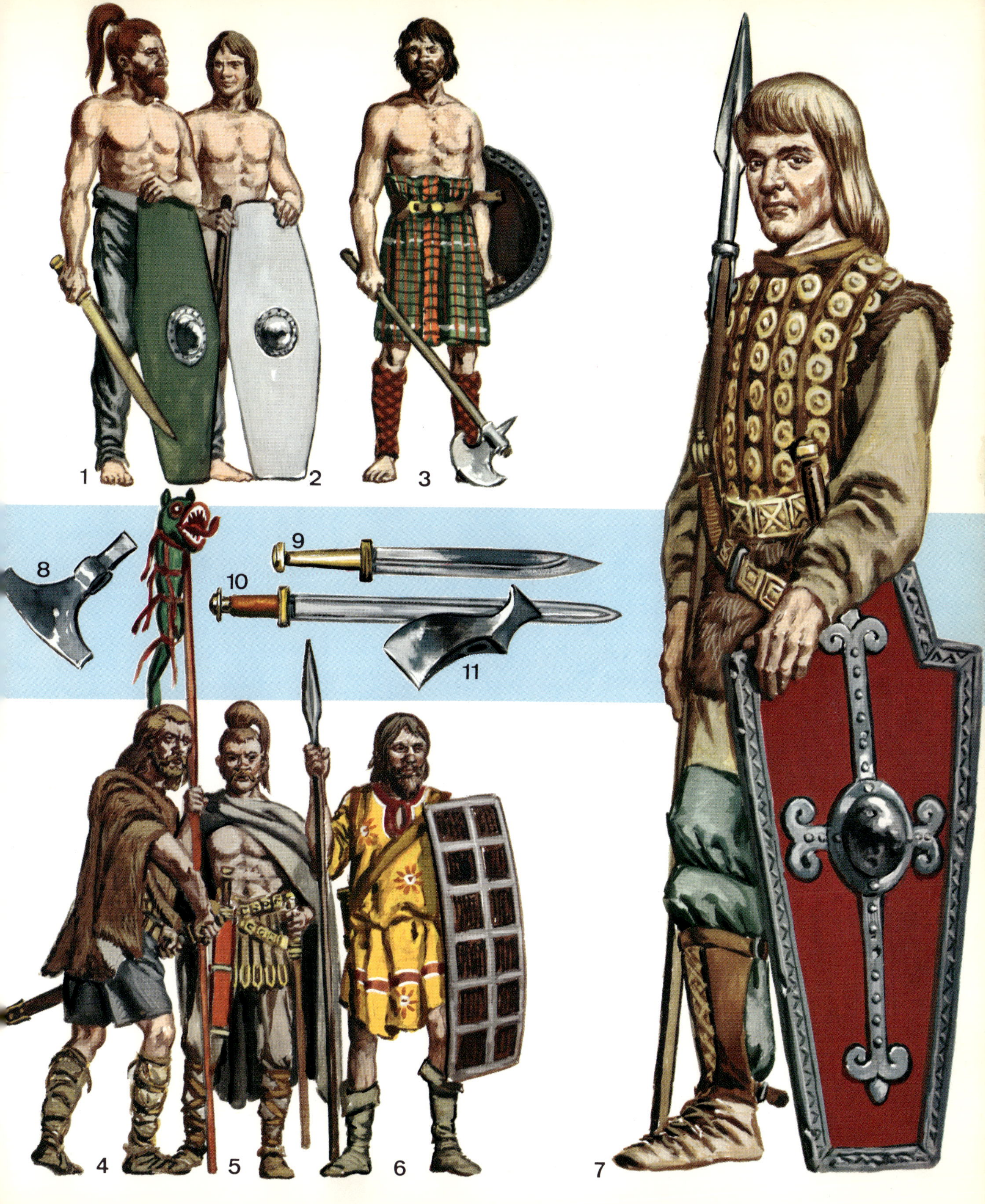
1
2
3
8
9
10
11
4
5
6
7

The Huns

Repulsively ugly, their hideous faces scarred by gashes made in their youth to destroy the roots of the beard, the Huns spread terror wherever they went.

They were a squat and powerfully-built people of extraordinary energy. The Hun spent practically his whole life in the saddle and was so hardened physically that he was quite indifferent to the comforts of home life. He fed on roots and raw meat made tender by simply pressing it between the saddle and the horse's back.

The Huns' favourite weapon was the bone bow, and they handled it with supreme skill. Their other weapons were a javelin, a heavy sword and a net, which they used like a lasso.

Their tactics were limited to furious charges and rapid withdrawals, and their victories were mainly due to their appearance, their fiendish howling and their mobility.

Beaten by the Roman general Aetius at the Catalannian Fields (Champagne), Attila and his warriors withdrew to Hungary – 'the country of the Huns'. The descendants of these terrible conquerors later spoke of them with as great a loathing as the Huns had excited in their own day.

In the 9th and 10th Centuries, the Hungarians ravaged the whole of Europe. They invaded France in 910, behaving just as had the hordes of Attila. They devastated Flanders, Alsace, Lorraine, Champagne and Aquitaine, driving onwards as far as Arles, so much so that their memory still lives in the popular imagination. It is these traditions that proved the subject of several of Perrault's fairy tales, and Tom Thumb's is none other than the 'ouigour' or 'ogour' of the 10th Century. The belief in the ogre's love of raw flesh also springs from the stories that the invaders drank the blood of their victims. The picture that has been preserved of the ogre is that of the descendants of the Huns, and the famous seven-league boots recall the lightning speed of their raids.

Already known to the Chinese, who suffered from their attacks long before the Christian Era, the Huns swarmed over Europe where they became the most feared and hated of the Barbarians. Their last great chief, Attila, dreamed of destroying the Roman Empire. With his death, the Hun hordes disappeared for good, but they left behind them memories that survive to this day.

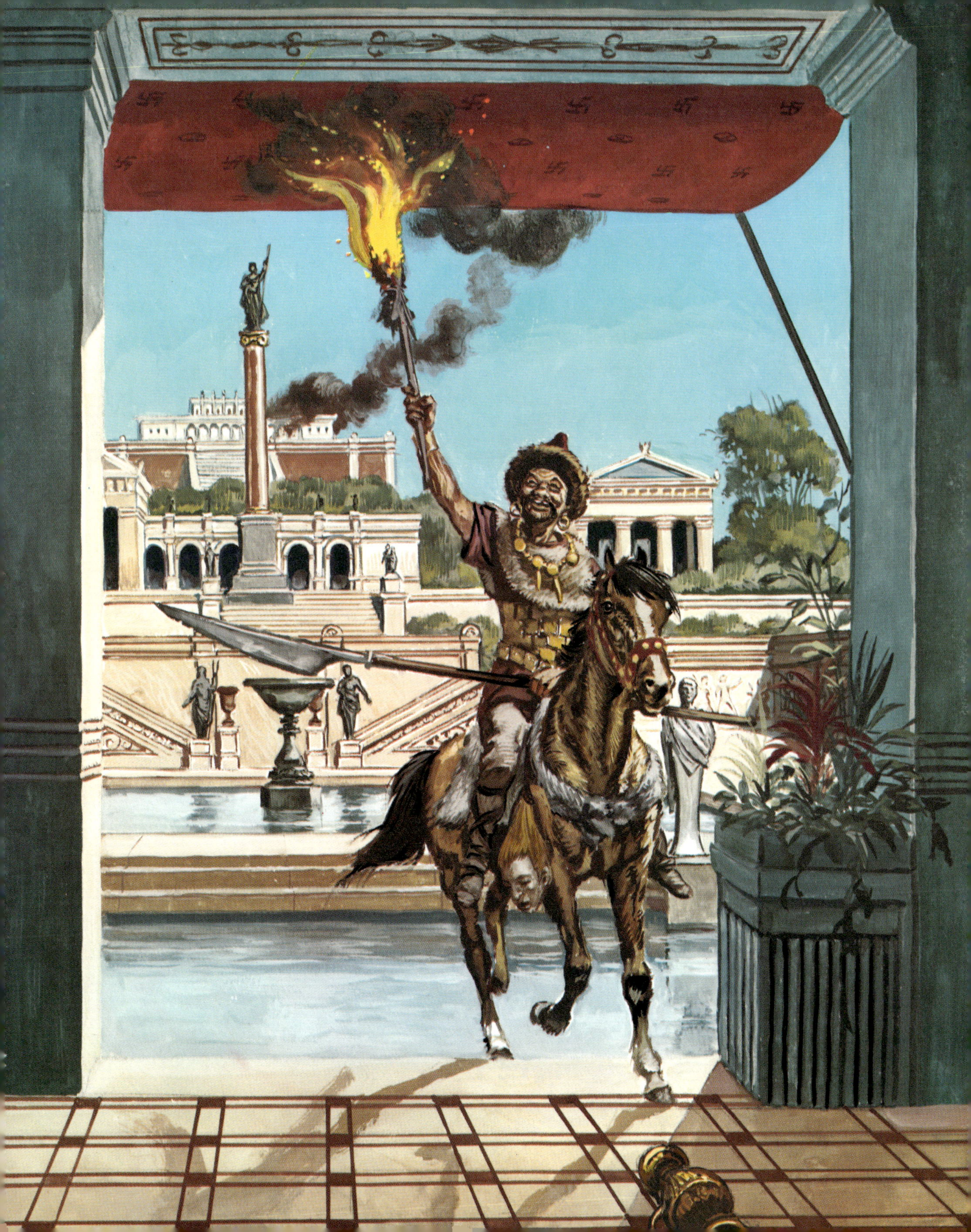

The Franks

The name 'Frank' appears for the first time in a marching song of the soldiers of Aurelius, who proudly proclaimed: 'We have killed a thousand Franks and a thousand Sarmatians; now we seek a thousand, thousand, thousand Persians.'

At the time of the conquest of Gaul the Franks were very simply armed. For personal protection, they had only a round or oval wooden shield[1] with a projecting boss in the centre.

OFFENSIVE WEAPONS

The Franks' offensive arms are well known to us thanks to the descriptions of them by Sidonius Apollinarius (450), Procopius (565), Agathias (6th Century), and Gregory of Tours (595), as well as to some important archaeological finds.

They were as follows:

1 The spear or 'framea', had several types of head which were secured to the shaft by a socket.

2 The barbed 'angon' was a javelin that could be used in hand-to-hand fighting or for throwing.

3 The 'francisca' was a throwing axe. The historians of the period have remarked upon the extraordinary skill with which the Franks handled this weapon.

4 The 'scramasax' was a large cutlass with a grooved blade on which poison was sometimes put. It was with a weapon of this type that the followers of Fredegonde perpetrated the crimes that gained her infamy.

5 The sword was flat, sharpened and double-edged, and seems to have been reserved to chiefs and chosen men. It was carried in a wooden or leather scabbard.

TACTICS

The primitive tactics of the Franks caused their crushing defeat at Casilinum, near Capua, in 553. The attack across close country against the enemy's heart was quickly halted; the enemy outflanked them, and massacred them to a man. Their tactics hardly improved over the next two hundred years, and consisted merely of butchering the local population.

[1] See note 2 on p. 60.

1, 2, 3, 4, Frankish warriors; 1 and 2 as described by Sidonius Appollinarius and Agathias. 5, spearheads and shield-bosses.

1
2
3
4

Anglo-Saxons and Carolingians

About the year 370, Great Britain, which was the northernmost colony of the Roman empire, was attacked from all sides. Led by King Arthur with his famous sword Excalibur, the Britons put up an heroic struggle against the Germanic invaders, the Angles and the Saxons.

Eventually they had to acknowledge defeat. Some sought refuge in the mountains of Wales and Cornwall, others fled across the sea to the Armorican peninsula and founded Brittany, named in memory of their lost homeland.

The great victory at Poitiers in 732 brings France on to the scene once more, for then Charles Martel restored the military glory of the Franks, at the same time putting in jeopardy the reputation of the Merovingian dynasty. It was he who saved Gaul and Europe from the threat of Islam.

To oppose the hordes of Adb-er-Rahman, he equipped his Neustrian and Austrasian troops with thick coats of mail and long spears. He hastily had made helmets composed of four triangular iron plates riveted together which, although they looked clumsy, were highly effective.

Adopting again the former tactics of opposing the enemy with a solid mass of men, but this time in open country that had been cleared, the Frankish chief waited calmly for the attack.

He waited seven days. When the Arabs at last decided to attack they could do nothing but dash themselves uselessly against the Franks' wall of steel. Only nightfall put an end to the massacre. At dawn, the Franks were still there, drawn-up in unbroken ranks, but the Arabs had lost heart and abandoned the field.

It is from Carloman (Charlemagne) himself, that we learn best about the military organization of the Carolingian period.

The most active of soldiers, he commanded his armies in person, leading them from Lombardy into Spain and from Spain into Germany, where the barbarian Saxons were setting out to pillage Frankish territory.

The cavalry, until then of little importance, began to play an increasingly important part during the reign of this great emperor, particularly as a means of bringing up reinforcements quickly to the furthest points of the empire.

Every free man had to answer the call to arms, but what was required of him depended on the extent of his lands. Charlemagne

1, 2, 3, 4, 5, Anglo-Saxons; 4 carries a horn for sending signals. 6, 7, 8, 9, 10, Carolingians; 6 is a body guard. *Upper panel:* Anglo-Saxon sword-hilts, axe-head and helmets. *Lower panel:* Carolingian sword-hilt, helmets, sword-hook, spur and stirrup.

87

laid down exactly in his *Capitulaires* the contribution due from each man. This was based on the agricultural unit, the 'manse' (15 hectares, or about 37½ acres).

According to the importance of the campaign, the emperor fixed the number of manses held by a landowner before he was liable for service at five, four or three. A man with only two manses had to pair off with another in the same circumstances and one went to the war while the other paid the expenses. Owners of a single manse were grouped together in sixes. Military service was compulsory up to the age of 60.

Apart from this national army, the emperor also had a bodyguard of mercenaries, equipped at his expense.

DEFENSIVE AND OFFENSIVE WEAPONS

Only rich freemen and big landowners possessed a full set of military equipment. They wore a 'brogne' or 'broigne', a leather garment reinforced with iron plates,[1] or a 'hauberk', a costly coat of mail. Their legs were protected by boots made of leather or iron, called 'bambergues'.

The round or oval shield had a pronounced boss in the middle and metal struts and rim. A helmet completed the defensive equipment.

Offensive weapons included the sword, with a wooden or leather scabbard covered with waxed cloth, the spear, the bow, and a quiver containing a dozen arrows and a spare bowstring.

TACTICS

Charlemagne, whose military genius was equalled by his genius for government, usually launched his troops at the centre of the opposing forces if they were divided into small groups. If they presented a continuous line, he attacked on one of the flanks, trying to drive it up against some natural obstacle; or else he destroyed the enemy's communications.

The siege equipment was similar to that used by the Romans, though with some improvements.

Carolingian warriors. The horseman with a lance is a soldier of the imperial guard. In the background is a fort with its 'dominium', forerunner of the feudal castle keep.

[1] p. 89.

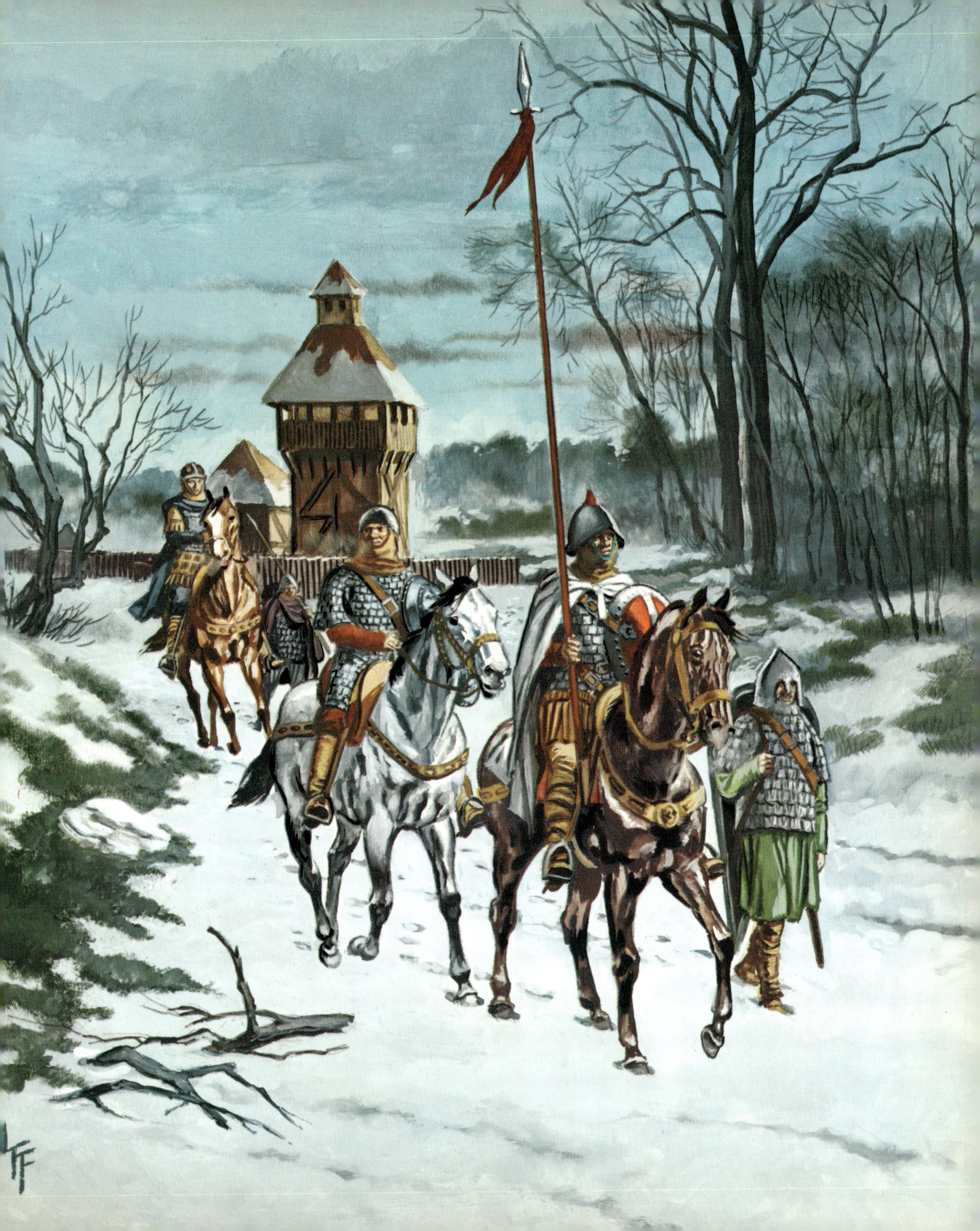

Vikings and Saracens

On one visit to the Narbonne region of Gaul, Charlemagne saw Scandinavian pirate ships operating under his very eyes, even venturing close to shore. When they were pursued they vanished over the horizon. Getting up from the table – so a chronicler tells us – the emperor went to a window that looked towards the east and stood there a long time in thought, his face wet with tears. Then he said to the nobles around him: "Do you know, my faithful friends, why I am weeping so bitterly? It is not that they trouble me with their miserable piracies, but that I am sorely afflicted to think that, while I am still alive, they have all but landed on these shores, and it grieves me greatly to think of the evil that they will inflict on my successors and their peoples."

The Vikings, or Norsemen, who had appeared upon the coasts of Gaul in 515 only to suffer a humiliating defeat, returned three centuries later, at the end of Charlemagne's reign.

These men, pursuing their bloody course, captured Ghent in 880. Louis of Neustria (Louis III of France) gave them battle at Saucourt-en-Vimeu, in Picardy, in 881. Nine thousand Vikings died on that field with their 'konong' (king or chief).

A little later, the Norsemen returned, greedier than ever, raiding as far inland as Cologne, Aix-la-Chapelle, Coblenz, and Treves, and even attacking Orleans and Paris, Bordeaux and Toulouse. Their insatiable appetite for booty drove them on into Spain and Africa. Other hordes, setting forth from Sweden, reached the Caspian, the Black Sea and Constantinople. Italy and Sicily were also struck by these tireless marauders, but it was the British Isles that suffered most at the hands of the Vikings, this time from Norway and Denmark. They also managed to reach the American continent, an astonishing achievement but historically of small importance.

The word Viking comes from 'Vik', cove or bay, and 'Ging', king. Their method of attack was to lie in wait at the entrance to the head of a bay for merchant ships sailing close inshore.

The Viking usually fought bare-chested. He wore a helmet with a crest in the shape of some animal, or one with projecting horns. His shield was oblong and his weapons were like those of other barbarous races.

As with the invaders from the North religion was the driving force among the Arabs.

In 711, they crossed the straits separating them from Europe. Their chief, Tarik, was to give his name to the rock where his forces landed, Djebel-al-Tarik (Gibraltar).

In about 720, they crossed over the Pyrenees into the kingdom of the Franks, and it was not until twelve years later that they were defeated.

Cavalry was the mainstay of the Arab armies. The horseman carried a round shield and wore a 'hoqueton', a padded and quilted smock, and sometimes the helmet had a spike on top. The curved and flexible sabre, skilfully forged (at Toledo), was his main weapon together with the bow and javelin.

The helmet and sabre often had religious inscriptions engraved on them, such as: "Succour comes from God and victory is near", or "There is no brave man but Ali, and no brave sword but Doulfekar".

In the 13th Century, the chronicler Joinville wrote: "The Saracens sent word to the Sudan by three 'messenger doves' that the king had arrived." This shows that the Arabs were versed in the use of carrier-pigeons for conveying despatches.

1, 2, 3, 4, Vikings; 3 is a chief. 5, 6, 7, Arab horsemen; 7 is wearing the quilted 'hoqueton'.

91

The Feudal Armies

Charles the Simple offered the Normans the opportunity of settling in his kingdom, hoping they would defend their fief against other marauders; so Normandy was born in 911. It was from there that a Norman duke, William, proclaimed himself heir to the throne of England in 1066, in spite of the fact that the Anglo-Saxons had just crowned one of their own claimants, Harold, brother-in-law of the dead king Edward the Confessor.

William began to recruit soldiers, promising them money or land in the kingdom to be overcome. They came to him from all over France, from Flanders, the Rhineland and Spain.

They were thoroughly trained for eight months. It has been estimated that the army numbered 14,000 men and 4,000 horses. The assembling of these animals is said to have led to the breeding of the present strain of Normandy horses.

In the mouth of the Dives (Calvados) they built the armada needed to transport this host. Historians have reckoned the number of boats at 696, each carrying 20 men. (The ancient authors talk of 3,000 boats and 60,000 men – obviously exaggerated figures.)

William weighed anchor on the morning of October 6th and landed on the Sussex coast. Astonishingly enough, he had brought with him three prefabricated wooden forts 'which were put up with lightning speed in a single day'. He erected one at the spot where he had landed, the second at Hastings – where Harold decided to fight him – and the third halfway between them. The king of England's army was certainly as large as the Duke of Normandy's, but it was made up mainly of 'fyrds' (peasant levies) surrounded by 'house carls', the royal guard.

The Anglo-Saxons had few archers and no cavalry; their principal weapon was the battle-axe, which was wielded with both hands.

But Harold had chosen his ground cleverly – a hill 80 m/268 ft high, its flanks well protected by ravines and marshes. On the morning of October 14th the two armies faced each other. William had deployed his troops in three sections, with the Normans in the middle. Each section was made up of a front line of archers, a second line of heavily armed foot-soldiers, and a third of horsemen – the knights.

1, Danish soldier at the time of the invasion of Britain. 2, Anglo-Saxon, early 11th century. 3, Saxon light infantry, 11th century. 4, Anglo-Danish soldier. 5, Anglo-Saxon archer. 6, Norman light infantry. 7, 8, 9, Norman soldiers. 10, 11, iron swords. The pommel and quillon of 11 is of walrus ivory. 12, spur. 13, bit. 14, 15, iron axe-heads.

92

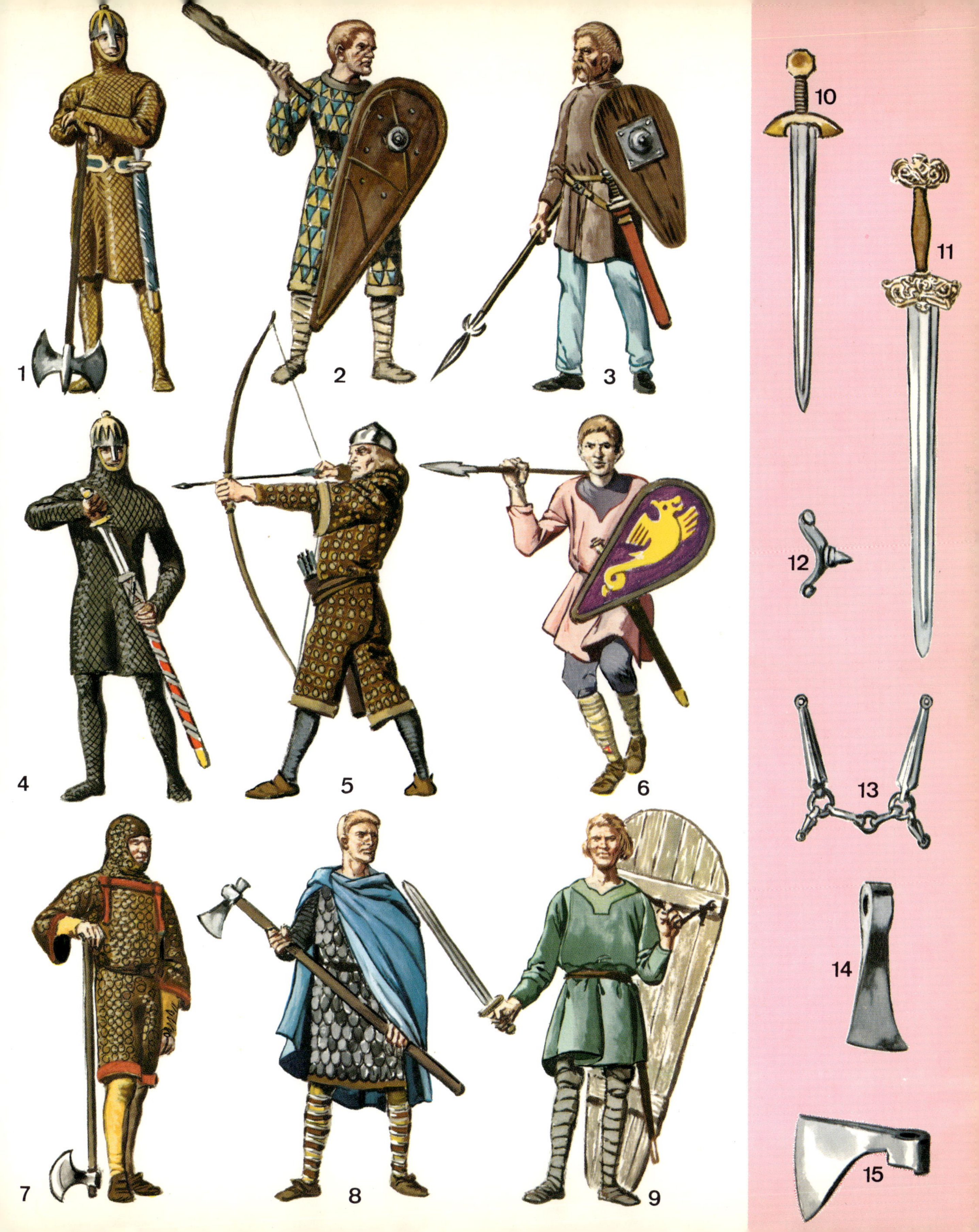
1
2
3
4
5
6
7
8
9
10
11
12
13
14
15

His archers opened the proceedings with a volley of arrows; it was immediately followed by a cavalry charge, which came to grief on the immovable wall of Anglo-Saxons. Another volley of arrows – this time shot into the air so that they fell vertically – created havoc amongst the English; one pierced Harold's eye, but he remained at the head of his troops. A second cavalry charge was even more ferociously repulsed, and the Normans came very near to panic. Seeing how useless were his efforts to break the English line, William hit on a strategem.

Once again he threw his troops into the attack, but this time he suddenly ordered some of them to withdraw, pretending this was the beginning of a general retreat. The Anglo-Saxons fell into the trap; breaking ranks, they surged forward. They were immediately attacked from behind by the Norman cavalry, and, in spite of a heroic rearguard action that lasted until nightfall, the English army was at last defeated.

The cumbersome double-handed axe (1·5 m/4½ ft long) so much loved by the Anglo-Saxons had one crucial disadvantage: it could only be wielded in a vertical plane. To lift it the soldier had to raise both arms – the moment the Norman was waiting for to thrust with his long sword.[1]

The Norman's body protection was far superior. The 'broigne' or 'byrnie', his thick leather tunic, was covered with plates or rings of iron and extended over his head in a mail hood.[2] It also protected him down to the knees.

The conical helmet, complete with nose guard,[3] was worn over the mail hood. A great shield gave protection against any pointed thrusts that might have pierced the byrnie, which in spite of its efficiency was still not perfect.

When he was using the lance the horseman sat up straight in the saddle so that the stirrups bore the whole weight of his body; in this way he got the maximum possible force behind the lance-thrust.

1 With the point. 2 p. 93, 7; p. 95, 4. 3 p. 93, 1/4; p. 95, 1/4/6; p. 97, 1/2/6/9; p. 99, 2/3/5/6.

CRUSADERS

1, 4, French. 2, German. 3, English. 5, archer. 6, Belgian crossbow-man. *Panel above:* swords, lance-heads and flail.

95

The Armies of the 12th Century

During the first half of the 12th Century, the byrnie was often reinforced instead with criss-crossed bands of leather, which made it lighter. It was then called a 'trellised' byrnie. From about 1150, with the beginning of the Crusades, the old coat of mail came back into use.

This new armour, reserved for knights, covered the whole body except the face. It was known as the 'hauberk'. With it were worn breeches covering the stomach, legs and feet; a padded lining was worn underneath which not only absorbed the shocks of blows but also served to prevent painful chafing of the skin by the heavy hauberk. Over it, they wore a tunic of some rich material, the 'gypoun', that, as well as looking decorative, stopped the armour becoming overheated in the sun. The hemispherical helmet had a visor with slits for the eyes.[1]

At the beginning of the 13th Century an extra part was added to the 'ventail' to give protection to the back of the neck: so the classical 'heaume' or 'helm'[2] came into existence. Underneath the eye-slits, ventilation holes were pierced, but nevertheless this heavy and suffocating accessory was only worn on the battlefield; at other times the knight made do with a sort of iron skull-cap called a 'basinet'.

At this time, horses began to be provided with protection in the form of padded cloths or blankets. The first spurs with rotating rowels came into use, though the old kind of spur was not abandoned.

The infantry was made up mainly of soldiers armed with longbows, crossbows and staffs. The Norman bow measured barely a metre. The English, who were famous for their archery, used a bow twice as long. The length of its arrow was about 90 cms/35 ins. The Italian bow was made of steel and was 1·5 ms/4½ ft in length, like the German bow. Longbows and crossbows were generally made of yew.

In the 13th Century, the bow was carried in a special case, and the arrows, sometimes called 'clothyards', in a quiver. There were many different shapes of arrowhead: one kind, in the form of a crescent (luna), was used to hack horses or to cut the cables of boats.

The longbow had an average range of about 200 m/655 ft. It owed its long popularity – at the expense of the more powerful crossbow – to its simplicity and accuracy. An archer could shoot up to a dozen arrows to the crossbowman's two or three.

1 p. 97, *7/8.*   2 p. 101, *1/5/10.*

Above helm 12th century. *Below* classical helm, 13th century.

KNIGHTS

1, 2, 3, French knights, late 12th century. 4, French horseman in leather hauberk, about 1100. 5, 6, 7, 8, 9, German knights, about 1200. 10, French knight about 1200.

97

At the beginning of its career, the crossbow was held in deep repugnance by the soldiers, who considered it a vicious weapon. One Lateran Council anathematized it, ruling that it was unfair, treacherous, and *artem mortiferam et Deo odibilem* (' a murderous art and hateful to God'); however they did not go so far as to forbid its use against the Infidels.

Richard the Lion Heart ignored the ban and armed his troops with the weapon when they were fighting Philippe Auguste of France. Curiously enough, it was a bolt from a crossbow that put an end to Richard's stormy career.

Crossbows of the early type were bent and loaded by hand, and were not very powerful; they were replaced in the 13th Century by the 'hook' crossbow, which was used until 1500. It got its name from the hook the crossbowman carried at his belt. To load it he would bend down and engage the string in the hook, then straighten his back to draw it up to the notch, at the same time putting his foot in a stirrup and forcing the stock[1] downwards.

TACTICS

The victory of Charles Martel at Poitiers had not put an end to the threat of Islam. In Spain, courageous Christians continued the fight to recapture from the Infidels the land of their ancestors; among them was the Cid Campeador (El Cid), who inspired the people with his example. But the Berbers were succeeded by Turks who had been converted to Islam, and these people took up the holy war again with renewed vigour.

They banned Jerusalem to Christians. Pilgrims had always been welcomed there by the Arabs, since they were an appreciable source of revenue, and this new measure gave rise to tremendous indignation throughout Christendom. Normans flocked to their standards to join the first crusade, but it was Godfrey of Bouillon and his brother Baudouin who were the first to raise an army, amongst the Flemings and Walloons. Eventually seven different armies converged on Constantinople, the general rallying-point.

The march on Syria began in the spring of 1097. To protect themselves from the intense heat, the Crusaders wore leather hoods over their helmets (silver-plated for princes, steel for others of noble birth). Their emblem was a red cross, usually sewn over the chest.

---

1 The stock of the crossbow which supports the bow itself and the release mechanism.

crossbow, 12th century.

crossbow, 13th century.

1, 6, French knights, about 1200.
2, Spanish foot soldier, 1190.
3, English foot soldier, 1160.
4, 5, French foot soldiers, early 12th century.

99

It was a victorious march. In the autumn they arrived before the gates of Antioch. The siege, which was badly organized to begin with, lasted eight months. The city-wall had a huge circumference and included four hundred towers. It was only when they managed to isolate the area completely, with the help of a strong palisade and two fortresses, that the Crusaders won the day.

The siege of Jerusalem began on June 7th, 1099. Helped by precious reinforcements of Genoese pioneers the Crusaders built mobile towers, battering-rams and throwing machines. The defenders hastened to strengthen weak points in the city's fortifications but the Crusaders changed the whole deployment of their machines in the course of a single night; then, attacking from three sides at once, they finally overcame the determined resistance of the Turks on July 15th.

The first two knights to set foot on the ramparts were the brothers Lietard and Engelbert of Tournai. The siege had lasted five weeks.

The Turks' tactics on open ground baffled the Crusaders. Their swift horsemen would harass the knights with bowshots, retreat before any attack, then regroup and fire their arrows again, repeating this ploy until the Crusaders' heavy cavalry were exhausted; then they would attack with sabres.

When the nature of the ground prevented this tactic, the superiority of the Christians was overwhelming. Thus at the lake of Antioch, Bohemond and seven hundred knights defied a powerful Turkish army by tying them down to a frontal combat in a narrow passage.

Eventually the Crusaders formed a light cavalry after the model of their enemy's. Since many of their horses had been killed – after Antioch only 700 of 70,000 were left alive – they replaced their losses with Syrian horses. They also opted for lighter equipment, changing their cumbersome and suffocating hauberks for 'saladins', light coats of mail from the workshops of Damascus.

The religious military orders date from this time. They built in the Holy Land splendid fortresses, several of which have been preserved intact to this day.

KNIGHTS (II)

1, 2, 3, 4, 5, French knights, 1200–50; 2 shows the cap (mortier) worn under the helm; 5 is wearing shoulder-pieces (ailettes). 6, 7, 8, 9, English knights, early 13th century; 7 is wearing shoulder-pieces turned backwards. 10, 11, 12, 13, 14, German knights, 13th century.

1 2 3 4 5
6 7 8 9
10 11 12 13 14

The Armies of the 13th Century

The closed helm, developed at the beginning of the 13th Century, soon underwent certain modifications designed to make it more practical; a movable visor was incorporated and the top became more pointed,[1] thus serving to deflect blows. But if the new shape proved effective in this way, it meant that blows aimed at the head were deflected downwards, breaking the knight's collar-bone. To get over this, special wing-plates[2] were fixed over the shoulders and attached by straps under the armpits. They formed an inclined plane to further deflect downward blows.

Mail was reinforced to give better protection against the steadily improving fighting techniques of the infantry. Plates of leather, iron or brass were sewn on mail to protect the shins, knees and elbows.

The sword became heavier and longer as defences against it improved. The horse was provided with a metal plate over the forehead, the 'chamfron' or 'chamfrain'. The infantry's staves, developed from tools used by the peasants in times of peace, gradually evolved into formidable weapons. The pike, handled by the people of Flanders and Picardy with such skill, gave rise to a variant with a hook for unseating horsemen; it was called a 'sackbut'. The hunting-spear was in fact a short pike. The ploughshare led to the war-scythe and slash-hook. The Swiss bill-hook was the model for yet another double-bladed, hooked weapon. The ordinary pitch-fork too was adapted for war.

According to the chronicler Froissart, the famous 'goedendag' used by the Flemings was a kind of mace as tall as a man and with an iron chain and point. But another writer of the 13th and 14th Centuries, Guiart, describes it as a coulter (ploughshare) mounted on a long handle.

Foot soldiers in the 14th Century carried a curved-bladed hybrid sword of Turkish origin. Since they wore no gauntlets, the sword had a Z-shaped quillon[3] to protect the hands and wrists.

In the Europe of this time, the duration of military service was only vaguely defined. In some parts the militia were not allowed to go on any expedition for their lord unless they could "go one day and return the next", a condition that severely restricted the warlike activities of some of the lesser nobility. Elsewhere soldiers followed their feudal master for as long as he thought necessary.

Helmet with visor hinged at side, 13th century. Helmets with visors pivoted at sides, late 13th century.

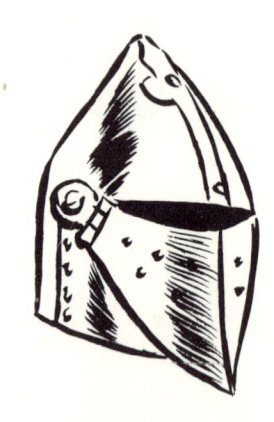

KNIGHTS (III)

1, French knight, early 13th century. 2, English knight, 13th century. 3, German knight, 13th century.

1 The part of the helmet above the skull.   2 p. 101, *5/7*; p. 107, centre.
3 The crossbars.

1

2

3

If any part of the territory of Flanders were at stake, the Flemings were forced to continue in military service until the coming of peace. Beyond the national border, the obligatory period was forty days, after which soldiers could quit the service of their sovereign, even in the middle of a siege.

TACTICS

In the 13th Century, a fighting army was generally divided into three groups: a centre and two wings, with the foot-soldiers ranged in several lines in front of the cavalry.

At Bouvines, on July 27th 1214, Philippe II Auguste of France joined battle with the combined forces of the Emperor of Germany, King John Lackland of England, and the Count of Flanders. The outcome was destined to be of great historical importance and made a single united France out of the French territories.

The French king confronted an army twice as numerous. Otho of Germany was surrounded by thousands of the pick of the knights from Saxony, Lorraine, Limburg and Namur. His infantry, fifty thousand strong, had been recruited in Germany and Flanders. The cavalry numbered ten thousand, including seven hundred English knights. The battle began with an attack on the centre by the Flemish forces – twenty thousand men advancing shoulder to shoulder and outnumbering the French by three to one. Seeing the danger, the Comte de Saint-Pol and his knights hurled themselves at the enemy and managed to break the Flemish ranks, in the middle of which the impetuous Philippe Auguste was now lying unsaddled.

The French knights then charged Otho, who had been exposed by the scattering of his troops. He only just managed to escape, carried off in his golden armour by a wounded horse in a headlong flight that did not end until they reached Valenciennes.

On the wings too, the French knights had triumphed, thanks to the skilful tactics they had learned through contact with the Saracens, and managed to stand firm before an enemy considerably superior in numbers.

The Flemings did not forget the lesson of that day. In 1302, their infantry once again met the French army, near Courtrai, in the Groeninghe Plain. Remembering the feats of their enemy's cavalry, they tried to render it ineffectual by taking up positions behind a stream three metres broad.

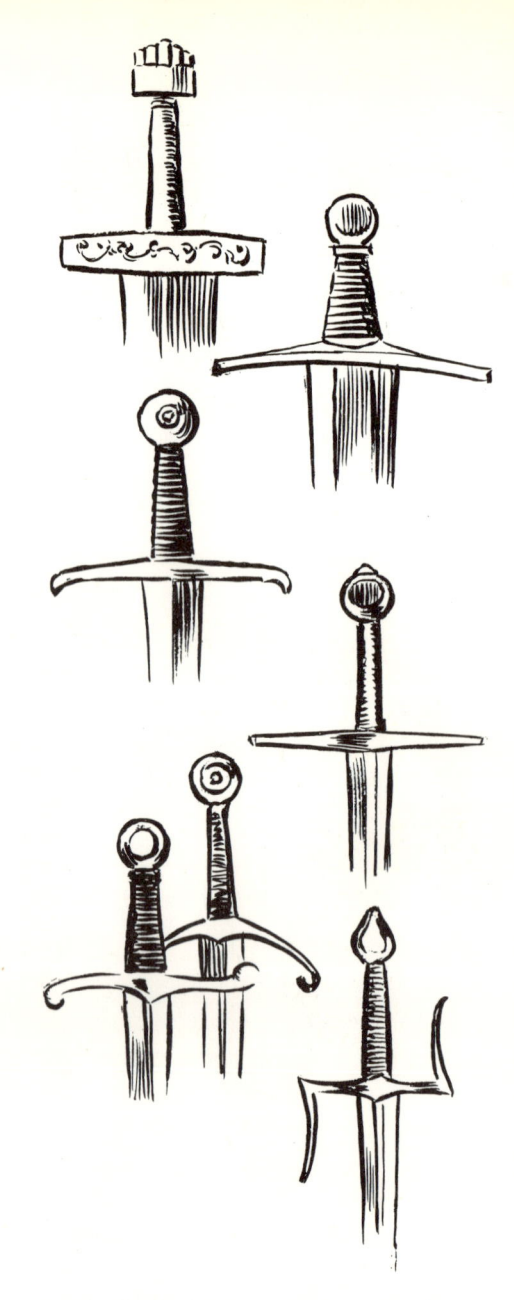

Sword hilts, 9th to 15th centuries. 15th century, with quillon in form of a Z.

1, 2, 3, 4, 5, French, late 14th century.
6, 7, 8, 9, 10, English, 14th century.
11, 12, 13, 14, 15, German, 14th century.

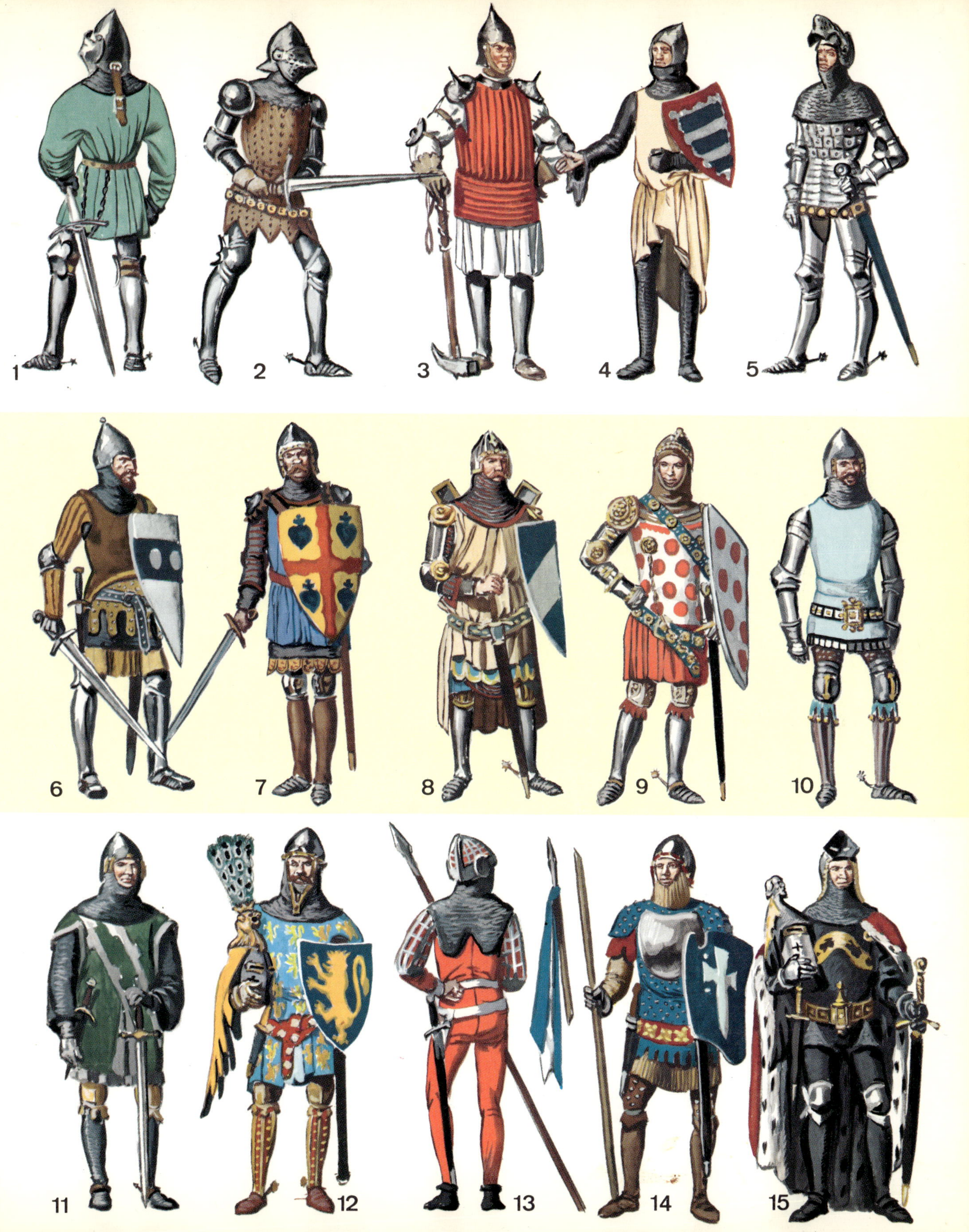
1
2
3
4
5
6
7
8
9
10
11
12
13
14
15

In the van of the French army were ten thousand foot-soldiers and Lombardy crossbowmen who opened the attack, forcing the Flemish archers to take cover behind their huge body of infantry.

Their retreat brought disaster to the French knights. Anxious to win all the glory of the day for themselves, they charged through their own infantry and attacked the Flemish centre, a position that happened to be held by inexperienced men who quickly broke and scattered. However, more seasoned soldiers from Ypres stopped their retreat and forced them back into the fight while the reserve hastened to the threatened position. The Picardy knights' moment of glory was short-lived. They were surrounded and massacred. The same reserve then advanced to relieve the pressure on the left wing. On the right, the Bruges contingent were holding their own against the furious assaults of the Frenchman Robert d'Artois. This magnificent warrior managed to fight his way right up to the Flemish standard and rip off a piece of it before being unhorsed. He demanded a nobleman to whom he could surrender his sword, but the ignorant soldiers did not understand the language he spoke. He was butchered on the spot.

Meanwhile, the whole body of French cavalry had made another charge, all discipline thrown to the winds in their impatience to join the battle. The result was appalling disorder. A host of them were unseated and died of asphyxiation in the bogs and swamps.

The two Flemish wings then closed in on what was left of the French squadrons, and there followed an interlude of wholesale butchery commemorated to this day by the name of the spot, Bloed-Meersh, the marsh of blood.

The Comte de Saint-Pol's rearguard fled without further ado. As at Poitiers and Agincourt, the French nobility had paid a terrible price for mistakenly putting the pursuit of glory before all else.

At the same time, we must bear in mind that, for the nobility, the cult of honour was the staple of their existence. Confronted with common people, nobles felt themselves bound to assert the superiority of their country, even at the price of glorious disaster.

It was the knighthood of England and Germany who first developed an effective answer to the tried and proved tactics of the infantry. When they were unable to force them out from their defensive positions, the knights dismounted and fought on foot. The practice continued until the creation of standing armies paid for out of public funds; in them the cavalry, formed into permanent units, assumed the role of supporting troops.

Knights of 14th century; in centre a bishop with a red mitre.

107

The Hundred Years' War

By declaring himself King of France and England, the young Edward III threw out a challenge to Philippe VI and set in motion a tragic war between the two countries that was to last over a hundred years, from 1337 to 1453.

In England military service was compulsory for every freeman between the ages of 16 and 60. Though poorly-off for cavalry, the English army had a numerous, well-trained body of infantry, at least half of it composed of the best archers in Europe. The other half were pikemen mixed with Flemish mercenaries. The English had taken advantage of the lessons learned at the battle of Bannockburn (1314), where the Scottish foot-soldiers of Robert Bruce had defeated the knights of Edward II.

In France, the crossbow had displaced the longbow, and the introduction of foreign contingents into the army had lowered its morale. The cavalry too had lost its effectiveness. Armour had got heavier and deprived it of mobility. Arms and legs were now enclosed in hinged steel 'canons', shoulders covered by steel 'epaulieres',[1] and the head by a 'basinet' with a 'visor' that opened sideways. From 1345 to 1360, there appeared close-fitting reinforced armour; Geoffroy de Charny, killed at Poitiers in 1356, speaks contemptuously of those knights who adopted such extravagant fashions and who, in order to appear more elegant, "make a habit of severely squeezing themselves in at the stomach".

From 1350 to 1390, armour was sometimes embellished by loose-flowing sleeves and skirts worn under the mail. These very impractical adornments led to the death of John Chandos, the only English knight to match the fame of the legendary Bertrand du Guesclin.

Surprising a party of Frenchmen, Chandos jumped off his horse to fight on foot. Froissart describes his death: 'That morning there had been a slight frost.[2] The ground was muddy so that, as he went along, he became entangled in his clothes, which were very long, and he stumbled a little.' At the same moment, a squire named Jacques de Saint-Martin dealt him a blow with his sword which

1 p. 107.   2 Hoar frost, it was a 31st December.

French knight, with types of swords and bassinets, 14th century.

108

109

he did not see coming, having lost the use of his right eye during a stag-hunt. It struck him in the face and before dying, Chandos begged his comrades to spare the Frenchman's life. He died the following day, January 1st, 1370. Chandos was Constable of Aquitaine and had come up against Bertrand du Guesclin on several occasions. An incident happened at the siege of Dinan, which was being held by du Guesclin, that well reflects the chivalrous spirit of the knights of the time. The brother of the French hero, Olivier, was captured by Thomas of Canterbury in defiance of a truce, and du Guesclin made his way to the Duke of Lancaster's camp to demand an explanation for this injustice. The Duke was playing chess with Chandos in the company of the Earls of Montfort and Pembroke and the famous Robert Knolles.

Hearing the grievance of the French champion, Chandos said to him: "If any man in our army has done you the slightest wrong, we shall immediately right that wrong." When du Guesclin challenged Canterbury to a duel Chandos offered him his horse and weapons.

The duel was fought in the presence of the leaders of both armies, and du Guesclin won. In his turn he treated Chandos with every courtesy.

Armour adapted itself to the pattern of incessant warfare, and what had been a series of separate plates developed into a system of jointed components.[1] Armour wrought in sheet metal had attained a very high standard and prohibitive prices for many warriors, who had to be content with 'brigandines' (jackets covered with laminated plates), or 'gambisen' (padded jackets). Plate-armour was known as 'white armour' because it was polished and without ornament.

The basinet replaced the 'helm' and 'tassettes' (thigh-guards) the old coat-of-mail. Epaulieres now protected the shoulders, armpits and shoulder-blades. 'Cubitieres' covered the elbows and articulated gauntlets the hands.[2] It was supposed that the perfecting of defensive armour would enhance the cavalry's diminishing reputation. The weight of this improved armour was such that it soon exhausted any knight fighting on foot.

Armourers reached the summit of their skill between 1430 and 1460 when they made suits of beaten metal no heavier than 25 kg/

1 p. 111.   2 p. 111.

ARMOUR

In centre panel: French suit of armour, 1440: A, skull; B, visor; C, air vents; D, pauldron; E, brassart; F, lance rest; G, breastplate; H, elbow cop; I, taces; J, tasset; K, fald; L, gauntlet; M, cuishe; N, knee cop; O, greave; P, solleret. 1, suit of armour worn by Bertrand du Guesclin, c. 1320–80. 2, 3, French suits of armour. 4, English suit of armour. 5, Italian suit of armour. 6, German suit of armour.

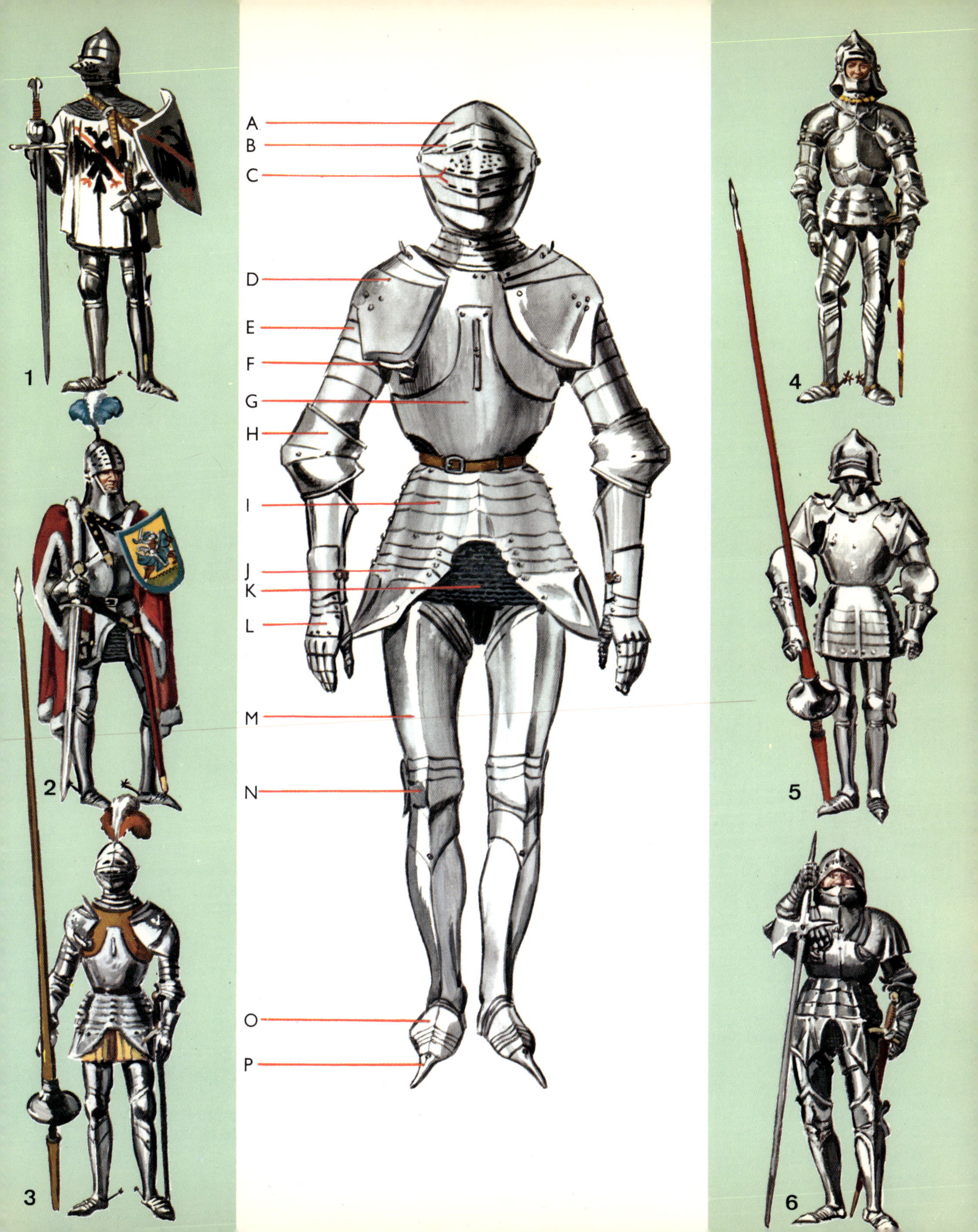

A
B
C
D
E
F
G
H
I
J
K
L
M
N
O
P
1
2
3
4
5
6

55 lbs. These suits were made of specially tempered sheet-steel beaten out very thin. The main centres of the armourer's craft were at Paris, Bourges, Ghent, Nuremburg and Milan. German armour was excellently made, though rather heavy, but the Italian was reputed to be the strongest.

Towards the end of the 15th Century a type of armour known as the 'Maximilian'[1] became fashionable. In this, the plates were fluted[2] to increase their strength, but the introduction of firearms marked the beginning of the end. Nevertheless, the tradition of wearing armour was so deeply rooted that men of noble birth would have considered it shameful to present themselves for battle without this cumbrous symbol of their nobility.

Artillery and Firearms

Artillery using the traditional forces of propulsion, the 'mangonel' and the 'trebuchet' (types of balista), and the crossbow, etc. gave place towards the middle of the 14th Century, to weapons using gun-powder as the propellant. In 1326, Florence was manufacturing cannon and shot. In 1356 the Black Prince, son of Edward III of England, used cannons at the siege of Romorantin. The weapon reached Scandinavia by 1360.

First made of cast metal, these cannon, known as 'basilisks', frequently blew up. Those of wrought iron were sometimes of a considerable size: the 'Dulle Griete' preserved in Ghent was about five metres long and had a calibre of 64 cms/25 ins; its shot weighed 340 kg/749½ lbs and it took a charge of 38 kg/84 lbs.

The earliest pieces were breech-loading.[3] At first they had a detachable breech, but later this was replaced by a chamber closed by means of a hinged breech block. Both mechanisms let

1 From the name of the emperor Maximilian.   2 Channels.
3 From behind.

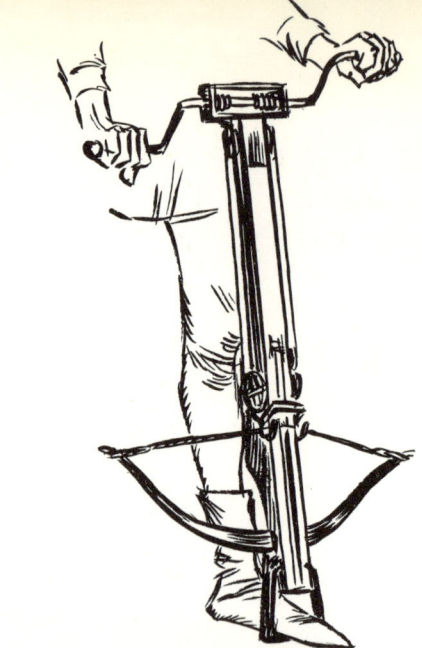

Two types of crossbow, 15th century.

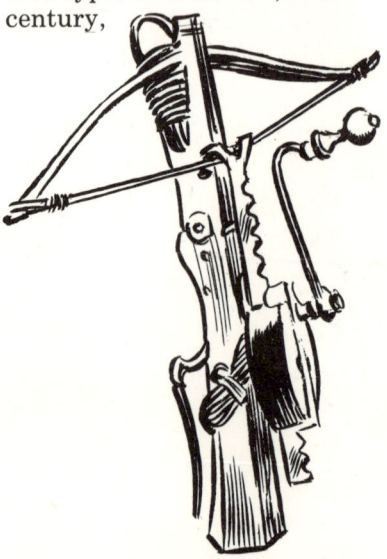

MEN-AT-ARMS OF THE LATTER PART OF THE 15th CENTURY

1, man-at-arms. 2, soldier with form of pike (coustille). 3, soldier with culverin. 4, mounted archer. 5, German man-at-arms, 1450. 6, crossbowman of the guard. 7, soldier with culverin, bodyguard of Charles the Bold, 1473. 8, archer, bodyguard of Charles the Bold, 1473. 9, archer of the guard (although this corps no longer carried bows after the reign of Louis XII, the old name was retained).

112

113

a great deal of gas escape. The problem was solved by casting the pieces in bronze, loading them at the muzzle and igniting the charge through a small hole, the touchhole, in the breech.

Towards 1450, pieces which hitherto had been seamed to their mountings with clamps, were mounted in carriages fitted with toothed racks, which made it possible to alter the elevation.

At the end of the 15th Century came the idea of moving artillery on wheeled carriages.

It is probable that the invention of the heavy weapons led to the idea of smaller versions. In any case, they were being manufactured at Perugia in 1364. The Germans called them *knallbuchsen* (pop-guns).

From 1400, hand-guns began to appear, 'culverins', complete with stock[1] and hackbuts. 'Hackbuts' had a metal lug or hook underneath that the firer could use to steady his weapon against a parapet. The hand-culverin needed a two-man team, one to aim and the other to fire. Mounted in a stock, one man could fire it. The hooked hackbut weighed 20–30 kg/44–66 lbs and needed two men to operate it. Until the beginning of the 16th Century, these arms remained inferior to the traditional missile weapons; they were very inaccurate and extremely dangerous to their users. They were more frightening than dangerous to the enemy.

Experiments were made to improve the primitive firing mechanism and protect the priming powder from the effects of wind and rain. Armourers devised the match-lock, which was simply an arm, pivoted on a metal plate, and carrying a lighted fuse that it dipped into the pan.

Perfected in the 16th Century, this device, which was termed generally the 'lock', was incorporated into the musket and arquebus and gave them an advantage over the earlier types.

1 They were fixed to a support.

1, 4, soldiers with firearms. 2, 3, light artillery mounted on carriages with rack elevation, mid-15th century. 5, French crossbowman. The English were distinguished by a red cross. 6, archer. 7, foot soldier with plommée. 8, man-at-arms with marteau-hache. 9, Italian foot soldier. 10, 11, 12, 13, early firearms. 10, Germany, 14th century. 11, Switzerland (1425). 12, Germany (1450), already resembling the modern shape. 13, Austria: mechanism with cock, early 15th century.

115

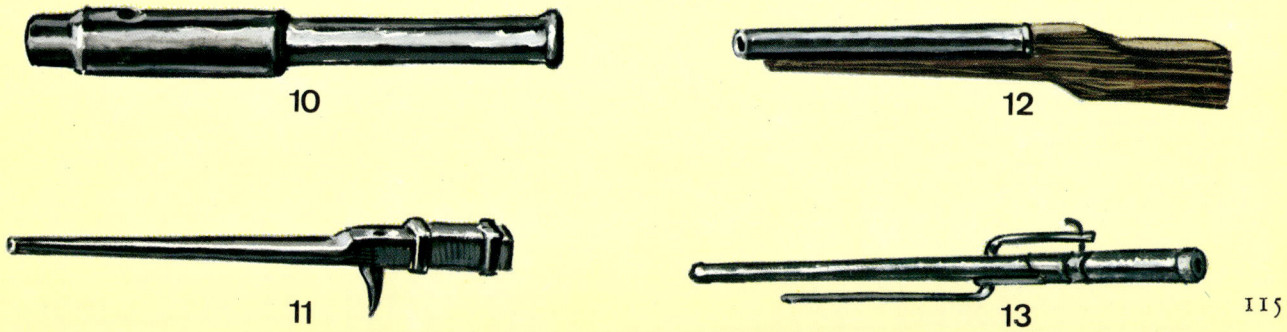

The Armies of the Renaissance

It was during the Italian wars that gunpowder established its supremacy and upset all the traditional ideas of warfare. The French were the last to adopt the new weapon: the 'arquebus'. Monluc wrote that it was only used by "cowards who would not dare to look in the face those whom they would strike down from afar with their miserable shot." Bayard, the last of the knights, was killed by a shot in the back from an arquebus.

A quarter of the Swiss and German forces were equipped with this weapon. The Spanish arquebusiers played a decisive part in the battle of Bicoque (1522) and Pavia (1525). Armour proved to be increasingly useless but nevertheless it was further strengthened, which only resulted in its becoming more inelegant. Charles V of Germany insisted on equipping his *gens d'armes* with complete suits of armour; he also paid his troops according to the amount of protective armour they had. If a soldier had a horse with no chamfrom, his month's pay dropped from 24 to 18 florins.

The offensive weapons of the cavalry continued to be the lance, five metres long, the mace and the sword.

At the beginning of the 16th Century the infantry still carried an odd assortment of weapons inherited from earlier centuries.

Arquebusiers were still held in contempt, witness the remarks of a 16th Century writer on military matters: "They were afraid to take a proper aim, for their weapon was like a short petard, heavy and clumsy, yet, for all its stout construction, it fired shot more suited to a pistol. The charge was ignited by hand, and the man turned his head away, jumping with fright when the arquebus went off. Indeed, it was more terrifying to the firer than to those for whom the shots were intended, and it's sheer bad luck on anyone who was hit, for he was unlikely to have been the one aimed at."

It was with such a weapon, however, that Admiral Leone Strozzi, who had introduced it into France, was killed by a shot fired from five hundred paces.

The infantry continued to carry a short sword, and a dagger at their hip.

1, Spanish man-at-arms, early 16th century. 2, Belgian arquebusier in the service of Charles V (1540). 3, German lansquenet with two-handed sword. 4, 5, Belgian pikeman and arquebusier. 6, 9, Turkish janissaries: they called the Sultan their foster-father, and their ranks were called after various appointments in the kitchen, 'great soup-server', 'master-cook', etc. 7, German lansquenet (1550). 8, officer, time of Charles IX. 10, body-guard, Charles IX (1562). *In centre:* mortar with aiming quadrant, and field piece, 16th century.

Match-lock and pan with pivoted cover.

117

Towards 1520, the hackbut, which had become lighter, was held steady on a forked support for firing. Later, it came to be known by its Spanish name of 'musket'.

There were two distinct weapons; the musket, which was supported at the muzzle when being fired, and the arquebus, which was fired with no other support than the hands. The skilful armourers on the other side of the Rhine devised the 'match-lock', which consisted of a pan (for the priming charge) with a pivoted cover, a movable arm which held the match, and a trigger which depressed the match into the pan. This mechanism, which was invented only ten years after the battle of Pavia, remained in use until the end of the 17th Century, and with it came the passing of the mechanically propelled weapons.

Artillery, too, underwent profound modifications. The weights of shot were limited to five – 40, 20, 12, 6½ and 3 lbs/18, 9, 5½, 3 and 1½ kg.

In France, Henry II limited the number of weights to six. There, artillery remained practically unchanged until the time of Louis XIV. As many as thirty-five horses were needed to pull some of the heaviest pieces.

During the 16th Century, the carriage was fitted with bearings[1] to take the trunnions that had been added to the piece, and the elevating rack was replaced by a wooden chock placed between the transom of the carriage and the breech.

Stone projectiles were abandoned for cast-iron shot. The foundries of Ciney and Dinant became famous, producing munitions throughout the 16th Century.

The gunner of the latter part of the 16th Century carried a 'linstock', a shaft fitted with a fork that held the match, which could also be used as a weapon.[2]

1, Belgian man-at-arms (1525).
2, German suit of armour (c. 1500).
3, light horseman (1540). 4, Spanish suit of armour (mid-16th century) with buckler for jousting.
5, suit of armour that belonged to Henry II of France (mid-16th century).

---

[1] Lateral pieces that supported the trunnions, some fixed pivots and the others to the gun.   [2] Shaft weapons are those whose iron piece is attached to a pole or support (pike, halberd). See p. 121, *11*.

119

Reiters and Lansquenets

The 'reiters' (German-horsemen), also known as 'black harness' and 'black devils', were mercenary cavalry of German origin. At first, they were taken into service by the Spanish and the Italians, and, then, from the time of the religious wars until the beginning of the reign of Louis XIV, by the French. They wore iron corselets painted black (hence the name 'black harness'). This was a device resorted to with poor-quality armour, for the paint hid the imperfections in the finish of the metal. The reiters sometimes stained their hands and faces, which earned for them the nickname of 'black devils' and also of 'barbouillés' (bedaubed).

Their most-used weapon was the pistol; they carried two in a double holster and aften a third stuck in the belt. An author of the time tells us that these pistols were "little arquebuses with a barrel only about a foot long, which were fired with one hand, the spark being made by a wheel (that is, the wheel-lock mechanism)."

The 'wheel-lock', which was a German invention, was an important modification. The match was replaced by a toothed wheel that rubbed against a flint[1] (like the modern cigarette lighter).

The reiters' method of fighting was highly individual. Formed up in quadrons of twenty to thirty ranks, each rank in turn fired their pistols, wheeled left, and galloped to the rear to reload. This tactic was known as the 'lunacon' or the 'caracole', and it proved highly successful upon many an occasion, but in the long run the reiters suffered so many losses that only a few returned to their native land.

The battle of Auneau, near Chartres (1587), was a particularly gloomy occasion for them. The moat surrounding Auneau castle was filled with the helmets – 'morions' and 'cabassets'[2] – and breastplates of the reiters killed in the fierce fighting.

'Lansquenets' derived their name from the German *land*, flat country, and *knecht*, servant (in contradistinction to the Swiss who came from mountainous country). Francis I had 4,000 of them in his service. Before him, Charles VIII had had 6,000 in his pay and Henry II, in 558, 20,000.

The lansquenets hired themselves out to the highest bidder, not hesitating to change sides in the middle of a campaign if the enemy offered them higher pay than their employer of the moment; or else they would demand double the sum originally agreed for their services.

Their tactics were simple: they would advance on the enemy, halberds at the port, drums beating. Before going off to fight, these bands of adventurers would offer up prayers, but their religious observancies ended there. In battle, they behaved like wild beasts. Their compatriots against whom they did not hesitate to fight, branded them as traitors and showed them no mercy.

Their bands were made up not only of Germans but also of Spaniards, French and Belgians, both Walloons and Flemings. After an expedition against the people of Ghent, twelve Belgians were hanged for acts of cruelty to their fellow countrymen.

The lansquenets said of themselves that one of their number who had been refused entry into Heaven was not even allowed into Hell, because his behaviour frightened even the Devil.

1 p. 121, *12/13*; p. 123, *12/13*; p. 125, *12*; p. 129, *10–12*.
2 The morion has an archedrim and is surmounted by a crescent-shaped crest; the cabasset has a much lower crest and a flat brim.

1, 2, 3, 4, 5, German lansquenets (no. 3 is a 'double-pay'). 6, 7, drummers. 8, reiters. 9, arquebus with match-lock mechanism. 10, arquebus with match-lock and revolver mechanism. 11, staff weapons. 12, wheel-lock pistol. 13, double-barrelled pistol. 14, powder horn. 15, reiter's pistol holster.

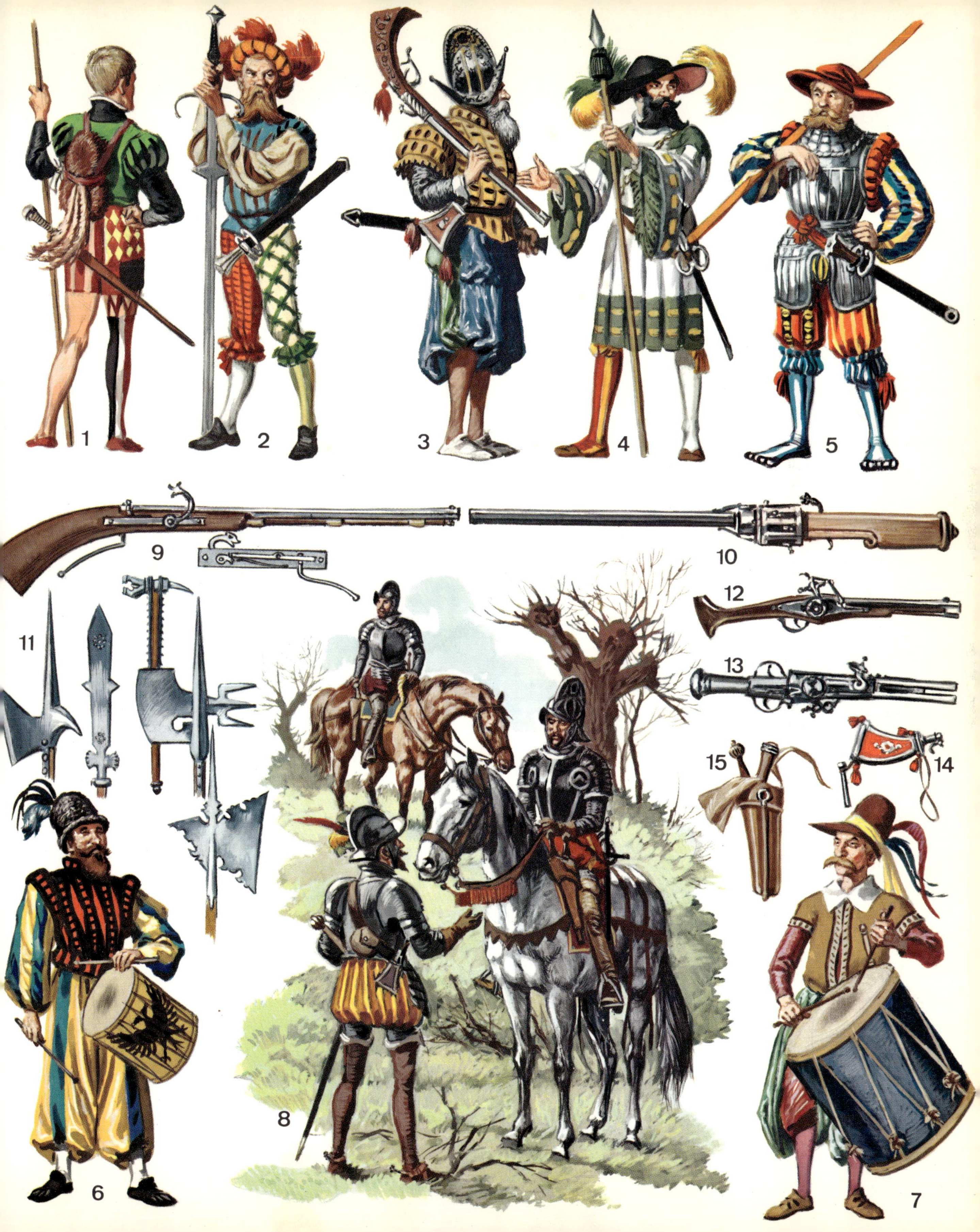
1
2
3
4
5
9
10
12
11
13
15
14
6
8
7

Mercenaries and Horsemen of the 16th Century

The French army at the beginning of the reign of Louis XII was made up of Swiss mercenaries, who were excellent soldiers, and lansquenets. Later, the Swiss withdrew from the French service, on the grounds that the pay was insufficient. Francis I took them into the service again, but eventually replaced them with regiments raised in Picardy, Champagne, Guienne, and Piedmont – the four original infantry regiments of the French army.

Italian mercenaries, practised arquebusiers, taught the French troops how to handle this weapon, although at first it was regarded with distaste. The Italians were adept at carrying out daring attacks, but they lacked the tenacity needed for long drawn-out operations.

The Germans were very good at fighting in open country, but slow to respond to the unexpected.

The Walloons were distinguished by their handsome uniforms. The Spanish were the finest soldiers of all. Tireless and well-disciplined, they excelled in ambushes, in fighting in close country and in the siege. The Flemings, the Scots and even the Poles also hired out their services to different nations.

The infantry of this time was made up of pike-men and arquebusiers. The German and the Swiss pikes were the longest, and the Germans, especially, handled them with great skill.

The heavy cavalry was made up of men-at-arms. They wore the cuirass,[1] a relic of the mediaeval armour – and their horses were protected by heavy bards. Because of the weight of this armour, which soon exhausted them, the horses were transported, when not in action, in wagons.

The light cavalry wore the arched-rimmed helmet, the 'morion', and carried the arquebus or a lance. In the second half of the 16th Century, the French light cavalry continued to wear the 'cuirass' as a protection against small arms fire.

The reiters, mentioned above, often won the day over an opposing heavy cavalry because, at point-blank range, their pistol shots pierced the armour of the men-at-arms.

Following the German practice, the cavalry charged at the trot. However, at this speed, the lance was ineffective, and in any case it made little impression on the increasingly heavy armour, so it fell into disuse.

At about this time, a hybrid mounted force, known as 'cuirassiers', was formed. They were armed with two pistols and a sword.

THE ARTILLERY

Artillery had made no progress in France. The Germans on the other hand had developed exploding bombs; they were fired from short gun-barrels. But the role of the artillery in battle remained a very minor one. At the battle of Houtain-l'Eveque[2] in 1568, the cannon of the Prince of Orange fired only five times and those of the Duke of Alba twenty-five.

1 p. 121, *5/8*; p. 123, *4/6*.   2 Or Walshoutem (Limbourg in Belgian).

1, arquebusier (1570). 2, fife player (1570). 3, Duke of Alba's Guard. 4, mounted arquebusier (1582). 5, body-guard of Philip IV of Spain. 6, French arquebusier. 7, Russian horseman. 8, Russian strelitz. 9, lancer of the body-guard, Netherlands (1572). 10, German mounted arquebusier. 11, archer, body-guard of Charles V (1543). 12, 13, wheel-lock pistols; 12 is fitted with a winder; 13 German (1577). These elaborate and costly pistols were used virtually only by the nobility.

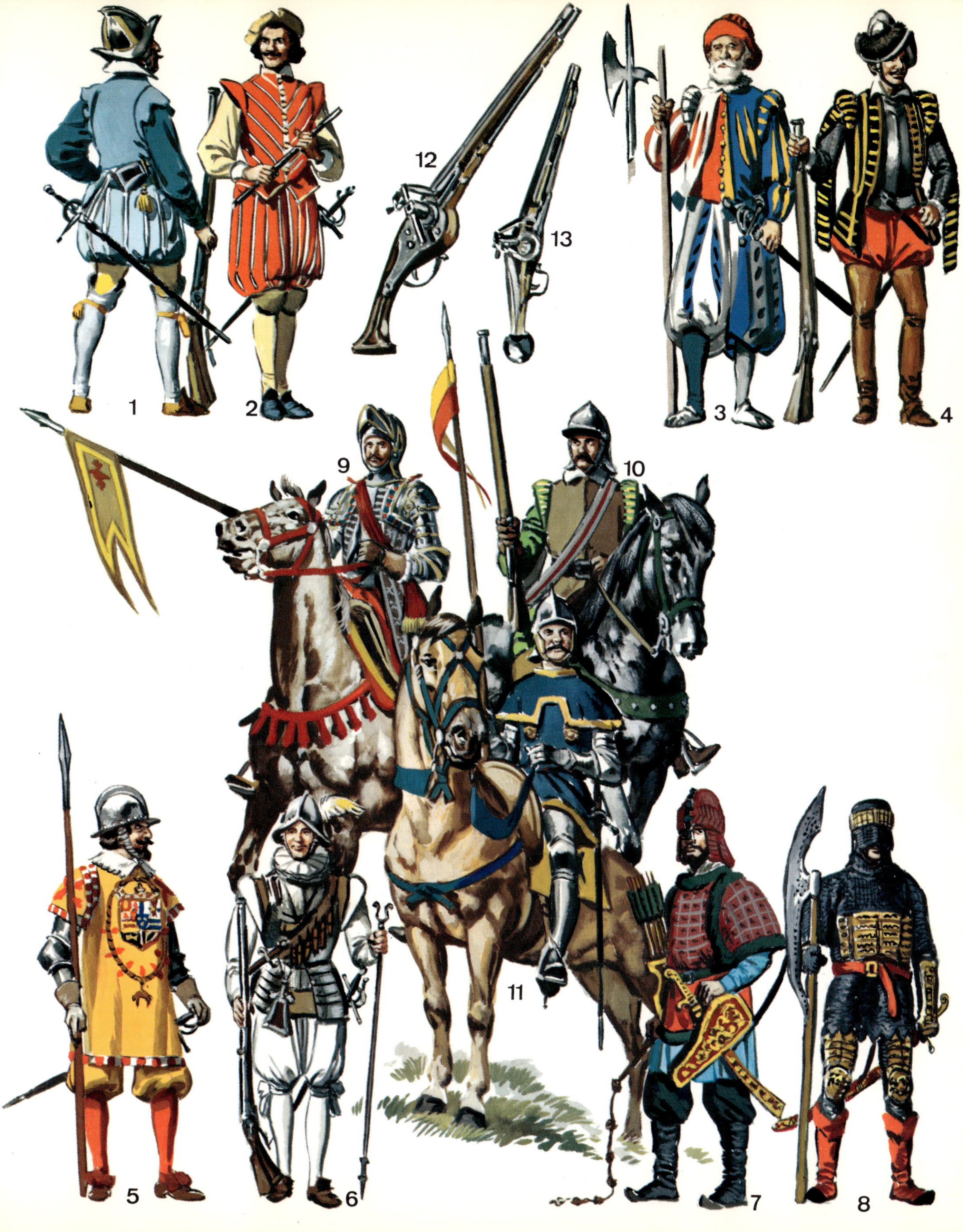
1
2
3
4
5
6
7
8
9
10
11
12
13

22 The Armies of the 17th Century

It was in the 17th Century that uniform first made its appearance, in 1632, with the blue, yellow and green regiments of King Gustavus Adolphus of Sweden.

In 1645 during the Civil War in England, Cromwell formed his New Model Army.[1] The troops, who were subject to strict discipline, were dressed in a red uniform and – a great innovation – they were regularly paid. The regiments drilled to the tune of hymns specially composed for the purpose.

In France, uniform was introduced only slowly at first. The results were very successful: soldiers looked well on parade, had no difficulty in recognising their own side in battle, and developed an *esprit de corps*. The example was later encouraged and developed by Louvois, the French military administrator.

The present system of military hierarchy also evolved in the 17th Century armies: the gamut runs from the private soldier with only himself to look after, to the corporal, the sergeant, the subaltern, the captain, the major, the lieutenant-colonel, right up to the commanders-in-chief.

THE INFANTRY

Foot-soldiers were the first to abandon heavy armour, keeping only the helmet and corselet. They were divided into pike-men and arquebusiers. Pikemen wore the helmet and corselet with tassettes (thigh-guards).[2] Arquebusiers wore the cabasset helmet instead of the older morion, and it was their only piece of defensive equipment.

Corporals were equipped no differently from the other soldiers in their sections; sergeants wore the morion, a bullet-proof cuirass weighing anything from 10–22 kg/22–48½ lbs, and carried a halberd.

Captains carried gilt, enamelled, or richly inlaid weapons. Sergeant-majors carried a measuring staff which they used to mark out the ground when drawing the troops up for battle. Commanders wore crested bullet-proof helmets, weighing 7–10 kg/15½–22 lbs and carried round shields.

The fully-equipped arquebusier carried a sword on his left side and a dagger or 'misericord' on his back.

1 p. 131, *4/5*.   2 p. 129, *5–9*.

THE THIRTY YEARS' WAR

1, light horseman (1620). 2, Dutch man-at-arms (1608). 3, Belgian dragoon in the Austrian service. 4, cuirassier, Regiment von Pappenheim (1640). 5, Flemish cuirassier in the Spanish service (1610). 6, French carabinier (1620). 7, Belgian lancer (1611). 8, 9, Belgian cuirassier and arquebusier in the Spanish service (1640). 10, arquebus. 11, musket, part-overhead view. These weapons could fire a shot about every five minutes. 12, German carbine.

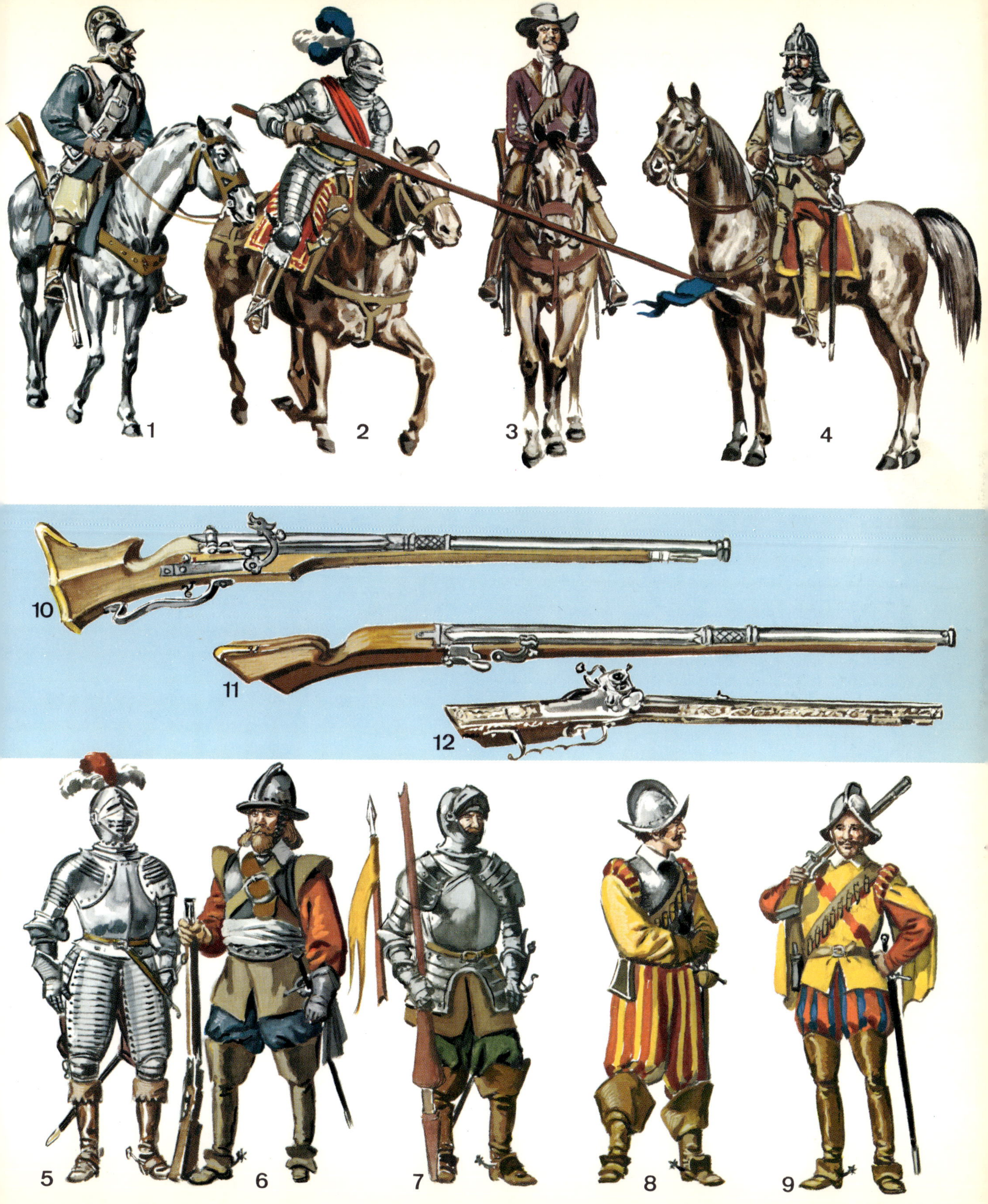
1
2
3
4
10
11
12
5
6
7
8
9

From the right side of his belt hung a leather pouch for his shot and attachments for two powder flasks, one containing powder for the charge, the other priming powder. He also carried spare fuses.[1] The musketeer only differed from his colleague the arquebusier in the calibre of his weapon and the support he carried for it. He usually wore a felt hat.[2]

Their main worry was to keep their powder dry. Cromwell used to say to his soldiers: "Put your trust in God, but keep your powder dry".

Pike-men received double pay, a term which became their nickname. Sometimes they were called corselets, after the name of their armour. Their pikes, of varying length, were made of ash. To face a cavalry charge, the pike-man would hold his weapon forward in his left hand, the point at the height of a horse's chest and the other end wedged against his right foot. With his drawn sword in his right hand he was ready to fall upon the horses as they advanced.[3]

Towards 1670, the first grenadiers appeared. They were specially selected from the infantrymen.

THE CAVALRY

The lance was still in use in the Low Countries and Spain, though in France it had disappeared in the time of Henry IV, because of the heavy losses sustained by the nobility of France in the Low Countries, which had reduced the number of gentlemen skilled in its use. Moreover, those who survived, ruined by the wars, had lost their best horses, carefully trained for fighting with the lance.

Their pay was insufficient to allow them to buy good horses, so most gentlemen were obliged to serve in the cuirassiers.

Armour, weighing from 35–40 kg/77–88 lbs, was worn beneath a leather surcoat that covered the whole torso. Many horsemen took advantage of it to shed the cuirass, retaining only the visible arm- and thigh-guards. This was discovered and the surcoat was replaced by a distinctive sash, worn over one shoulder. The colour varied according to the country; in England it was blue, in Holland orange, in Spain red, and, according to their party, in France white or black.

The cavalry that retained the cuirass, the 'cuirassiers', had to withstand the shock of the enemy pikemen. They were armed with swords, and their horses were common property. In battle, it was usual to place at their head the most seasoned soldiers, whose cuirasses were bullet-proof. These men received a bonus of 10% of their pay.

1 p. 119, *2/5*; p. 123, *1/4/6*; p. 125, *9*.   2 p. 133, *1/2/5–9/12*.
3 p. 129, *6*.

1, cuirassier (1640). 2, Savoyard helmet (16th century). 3, cuirassier (1610). 4, lancer (1638). 5, lancer's pistol holster. 6, cuirassier's pistol holster. 7, dragoon (1616). 8, suit of armour that belonged to Louis XIII. 9, Italian pistols (1680).

127

Mounted arquebusiers carried their weapon on a belt over the shoulder. They rode medium-sized fast horses.

The wheel-lock arquebus was accurate up to a range of three hundred paces [78 m/250 ft].

Dragoons first appeared in England during the Civil War.[1] In 1615, Walhousen, in his work *L'Art militaire a cheval* describes the dragoons as mounted infantry intended to support the cavalry.

In Germany, the dragoons were drawn half from the musketeers and half from the pike-men, and both carried the normal equipment of the foot soldier. In France and elsewhere, they were drawn only from the musketeers.

THE DEVELOPMENT OF FIREARMS

With the disappearance of heavy armour the musket became lighter and a support was no longer needed when firing.

Wheel-lock weapons were gradually replaced by 'flint-lock' weapons, and, from 1678, all cavalry were equipped with them. The wheel-lock had gone out of use completely by 1700.

The first type of flint-operated firing mechanism, the 'miquelet-lock',[2] was invented in Spain at the end of the 16th Century. An improved version, the flint-lock,[3] was soon introduced in France and Italy. This permitted of the musket being fired from the shoulder, instead of the chest, which allowed of more accurate aim being taken. Nevertheless the musket support continued in use in Germany until the end of the 17th Century.

With the development of firearms came a reduction in the number of pike-men, who disappeared completely with the invention of the bayonet.[4] This is said to have been invented in Bayonne about the year 1674, but French soldiers were already using a 'bayonet' with a hand-grip in 1642, and it was adopted by the Dutch in 1647. It seems more likely to have derived its name from the Roman 'baynata', little scabbard, on the principle that the container gave its name to what it contained. The first bayonet scabbards were of beautifully worked leather.

In the campaign in Flanders in 1642 M. de Puysegur mentioned soldiers armed with bayonets 1 ft/30 cms long, the hilts of which plugged into the muzzle of the musket. The blade of this weapon was shaped like that of a halberd, double-edged[5] and sharpened to a point.

1 p. 131, *5.*   2 p. 143, *18.*   3 p. 143, *19.*   4 p. 143, *11/15/16/17.*   5 p. 143, *11*; p. 141, *8/11–13.*

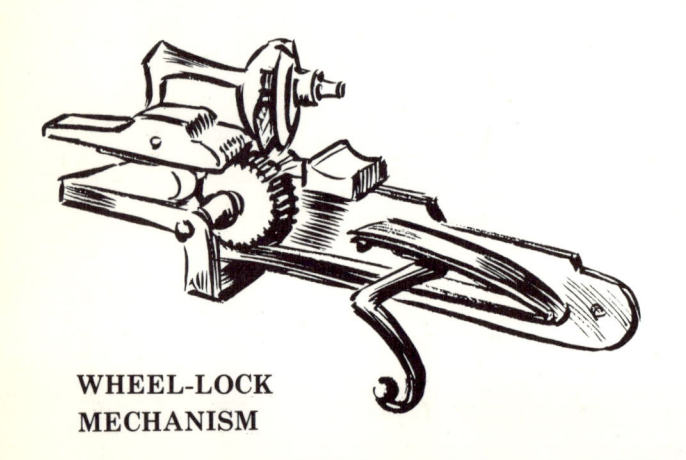

WHEEL-LOCK MECHANISM

1, pikeman (early 16th century). 2, gunner with linstock (16th century). 3, Walloon ensign (with colour) in the Spanish service (1640). 4, Walloon arquebusier in the Spanish service (1640). 5, 6, 7, 8, 9, pikemen performing pike drill. 10, 11, pistols of the time of Louis XIII. 12, pistol of the time of Charles V. 13, capeline, cavalry. 14 cabasset, infantry.

128

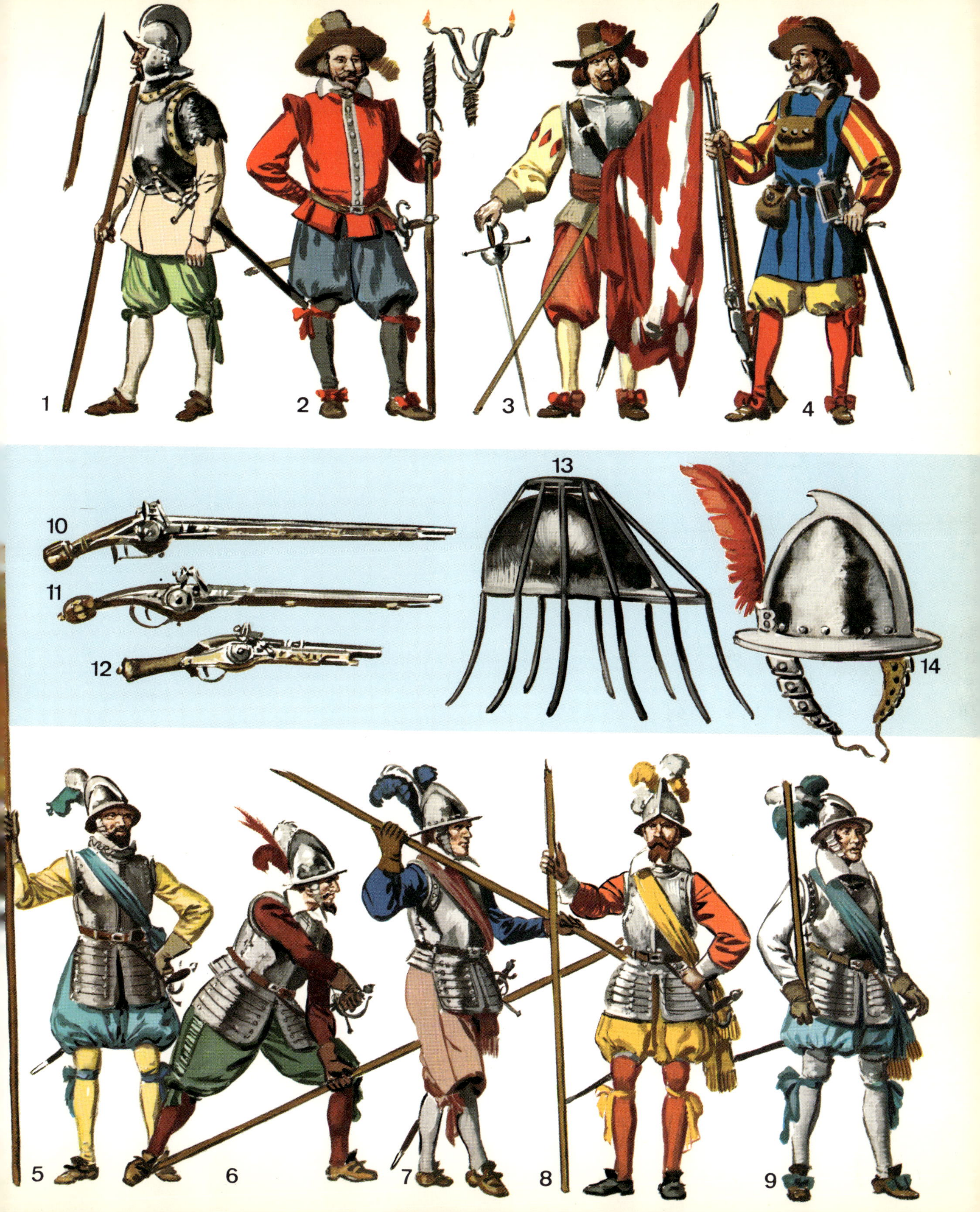
1
2
3
4
10
11
12
13
14
5
6
7
8
9

The French Regiment of Fusiliers were issued with the bayonet in 1671, and the dragoons in 1676. Two years later, the grenadiers were equipped with it. It seems to have been adopted by the English in about 1662, probably having been introduced from France. The English infantry and dragoons were issued with bayonets in 1673. Then, it disappeared for a time, but came back for good in 1686. By the end of the 17th Century, the entire English army had the bayonet. In the meantime, in 1689, there had been an important improvement; the grip had been replaced by two rings by which it could be attached to the barrel and still allow the musket to be fired.

Another type, the socket bayonet,[1] was invented in 1681. This was perfected in 1689 by the Scottish general, Donald Mackay, and became the standard model. The French army had introduced this modification sometime before.

The 'cartridge', invented in Spain about 1567 and appeared in Italy from 1597, only became generally used in 1644. The self-contained charge was a most important advance over the old method, which involved a whole series of accessories.

The cartridge-pouch[2] dates from the same period. It had originally been devised by the Swedish strategist, King Gustavus Adolphus.

At the end of the century, a new type of musket was introduced in Germany. In 1681, an Austrian general, named Montecuculli, invented the fusil musket, which combined the match-lock and the flint-lock. The latter was used for fighting at night or in wet weather, because the glowing match was too conspicuous in the dark and too easily put out by rain. The weapon became so popular that, after the battle of Steenkirk in 1692, the French soldiers left their muskets behind on the field and picked up the fusil muskets abandoned by the Allies.

At this time, too, the famous French military engineer Vauban equipped his army with a musket of the same type.[3] It was invented by him and called the 'Vauban fusil'. However, it was quickly superseded as further improvements were made.

Muskets were fitted with slings in 1685,[4] but only for the grenadiers, who needed both hands free for throwing their grenades, which were ignited with a match.

WEAPONS

With the adoption of uniform, weapons too became standardized and the specifications of swords and pikes and the calibre of firearms were laid down.

1 p. 143, *15–17*.　2 p. 141, *1–2/7–8/11–13*.　3 p. 143, *13*.
4 p. 141. *8*.

Miquelet-lock: the mechanism was on the outside and was unprotected.

Flint-lock.

ENGLAND DURING THE CIVIL WAR
1, officer, Royalist cavalry. 2, Royalist cuirassier. 3, cornet (with standard). 4, horseman, Parliamentarian army. 5, dragoon, Cromwell's Ironsides. These troops received a high rate of pay, which served to restrain them from looting and desertion. The Royalist troops, who were badly paid and poorly disciplined, suffered numerous defeats.

131

THE ARTILLERY

At the beginning of the 17th Century, artillery-pieces had a large number of different calibres, which led to difficulties in the manufacture and supply of munitions.

The Spanish reduced the numbers of weights of shot to four. Their heaviest pieces weighed over 3 tons/3,050 kg and fired a shot of 40 lbs/18 kg; the smallest weighed 1,500 kg/3,307 lbs and fired a shot of 5 lbs/2·3 kg. They were mounted on special light carriages, but, even then required teams of up to twenty-four draught horses. Wagons were requisitioned for the artillery train carrying their powder and shot.

Before loading, the gunner inspected the piece to make sure that it was not cracked. Then, he cleaned out the bore with a dry brush,[1] before putting in the powder with a long handled scoop and pushing home a straw wad. Next, he brushed out the bore to remove any loose powder, and rammed home the shot which had been cleaned and packed with tow. Finally, he primed the gun with fine powder, and it remained only for him to put the match to the touch-hole.

After the gun had been fired, he swabbed the barrel out with a sheepskin sponge dipped in a mixture of water and vinegar. Eight to ten shots an hour could be fired. Sometimes, instead of loose powder, ready-made charges in cloth bags were used. After the charge had been put in the gun the bag was pierced through the touch-hole.

TACTICS

Gustavus Adolphus, one of the greatest soldiers of the 17th Century, made a number of important changes in the tactics of the day.

Two-thirds of his infantry were musketeers, and he improved their fire power by issuing them with cartridges. The cavalry were also issued with fire-arms. The heavy artillery was placed in the front line, with the light artillery in support.

The same tactics were adopted by other countries, and battles generally started with lengthy artillery duels that went on for several hours until one or other side was completely silenced. This, it was thought, achieved great tactical and psychological advantage (though whether it really did is open to doubt), and the troops then advanced in open order, often having to halt to reform because of the nature of the ground or losses due to enemy fire. The artillery had to follow this slow advance as best they could, continuing to support the attack with

1 p. 141, *9*.

1, 2, 3, 4, 5, 6, 7, the arquebus. 8, 9, 10, 11, 12, the musket. The figures of different nationalities and dates, show various positions. 1, France, musketeer, Royal Household. 2, France, musketeer, Cardinal's Household. 3, England, arquebusier, Royalist army (1642). 4, Scots Highlander. 5, England, arquebusier, time of Charles II. 6, England, Parliamentarian soldier. 7, Walloon. 8, Fleming. 9, Walloon in the Spanish service (1690). 10, Frenchman. 11, England, foot guard (1660). 12, Dutch (1691).

133

fire. Usually, however, only a few guns managed to keep up. Consequently, the troops reached the enemy positions with practically no support and well within range of their guns, which inflicted heavy losses with grape-shot![1] Only the arrival of the attacking artillery could restore the situation.

The advantage thus lay with the defenders, and one can well understand why the generals of this period relied upon the artillery duel for the success of an action.

THE BATTLE OF ROCROY

On May 19th, 1643, the reputedly invincible Spanish army suffered its first major defeat.

Don Francisco de Mello, Governor of the Low Countries, had determined to seize the town of Rocroy, and accordingly laid siege to it in the spring of that year with an army of 27,000 men.

Louis XIII had just died, and the twenty-two-year-old son of the Prince of Condé opened the reign of the Sun King with a master stroke. The young Duke of Enghien[2] drew up his army of 14,000 foot and 6,000 horse soldiers and attacked the redoubtable Spanish tercios.

Inspired by the lessons of Gustavus Adolphus, Enghien created a mobile and flexible force of infantry made up of alternate groups of pike-men and arquebusiers. From the unruly and disordered cavalry, he built up a disciplined force. His artillery, like that of the Spaniards, was much weakened by continuous campaigning. He could only field twelve pieces against the Spaniards' eighteen.

The French army was deployed on a front of 2·5 kms/1½ miles in face of the Spanish. The infantry was in the core and the cavalry on the flanks.

The action began with an attack by the French right wing. Here the French cavalry got the better of the Spaniards, but, on the other wing, another French attack was broken by the Spanish cavalry, who then charged the French infantry and captured the batteries drawn up as usual in front.

The French foot-soldiers started falling back before the onslaught of the enemy cavalry, who were already claiming victory. Would Enghien abandon the advantage won on his right flank and go to the support of his left? Trusting in his luck, he outflanked the Spanish infantry and attacked with most of his cavalry in the rear. Meanwhile, the French reserve under Sirot, another student of Gustavus Adolphus, reinforced the threatened centre and held the attack, and, in the process recaptured the guns taken by the Spanish and manhandled them into new positions.

[1] With the bits of scrap metal or iron.
[2] The future Grande Condé (1621–1686).

INFANTRY OF LOUIS XIV

1, body-guard (1672). 2, sergeant (1674). 3, fusilier, Regiment of Picardy. 4, 5, officers. 6, corporal. 7, ensign, Regiment of Fusiliers of the King. 8, ensign, Regiment of Carignan-Sallières (1665). 9, ensign, Regiment of the Admiral of France (1670). 10, marine (1697). 11, fusilier of the Guard. 12, Swiss guard. 13, 14, 15, soldier, drummer and fife player (1672).

135

The Spanish tercios, described by the French writer Bossuet as: "huge battalions in close formation that resembled so many solid towers, but towers with the ability to repair themselves when damaged", put up a stout resistance. Enghien realized that victory would not be his unless they were completely destroyed.

Three times, his attacks were repulsed by the Spaniards' and Walloons' regiments. Then the young French commander consolidated for a fourth attack, and finally won the day. Disorganized, the Spanish surrendered, but only after a desperate fight. Their commander, the Belgian Comte de Fontaine, was killed at their head. The Spanish army lost 8,000 killed and 7,000 prisoners. It never recovered from the blow which destroyed its prestige as well as its manpower.

It has been suggested, with some justification, that the Spanish tercios were defeated because many of their best men had been taken for service in Germany and Catalonia. The cavalry, for their part, had fought without spirit, because they resented being commanded by a foreigner, the Count of Albuquerque.

However this may be, the outcome of the battle proved a triumph for the audacious young commander and his mobile and well-disciplined army over the sheer weight of numbers of the enemy.

ATTACKING AND DEFENDING FORTIFIED POSITIONS

The wooden keep of the early Middle Ages and the stockade and mound, these were succeeded by stone castles in the 10th Century and in the course developed into the true fortress.

The invention of artillery upset all earlier concepts of fortifications and siege-works.

We must not assume from this, however, that the former citadels were therefore abandoned as of no further use. Their massive walls could stand up to the heaviest bombardment and, indeed, they proved such effective refuges for the enemies of Cardinal Richelieu in the middle of the 17th Century that he was forced to raze them to the ground. This in itself proves their military value.

The first improvements in the defence works of fortified towns originated with the Italian military engineers who added bastions and casements to the simple curtain wall making it possible for the defenders to bring cross-fire to bear. Their example was soon copied by the French, notably Jean Errard, the father of fortification in France, whose treatise *Fortification in Principle and Practice* was translated into several languages and even appeared in pirated editions.

CAVALRY OF LOUIS XIV
1, dragoon (1684). 2, trooper, Regiment of Praslin (1693). He wears his cuirass under his coat. 3, hussar (1700). 4, carabinier (1684). 5, cuirassier (1668).

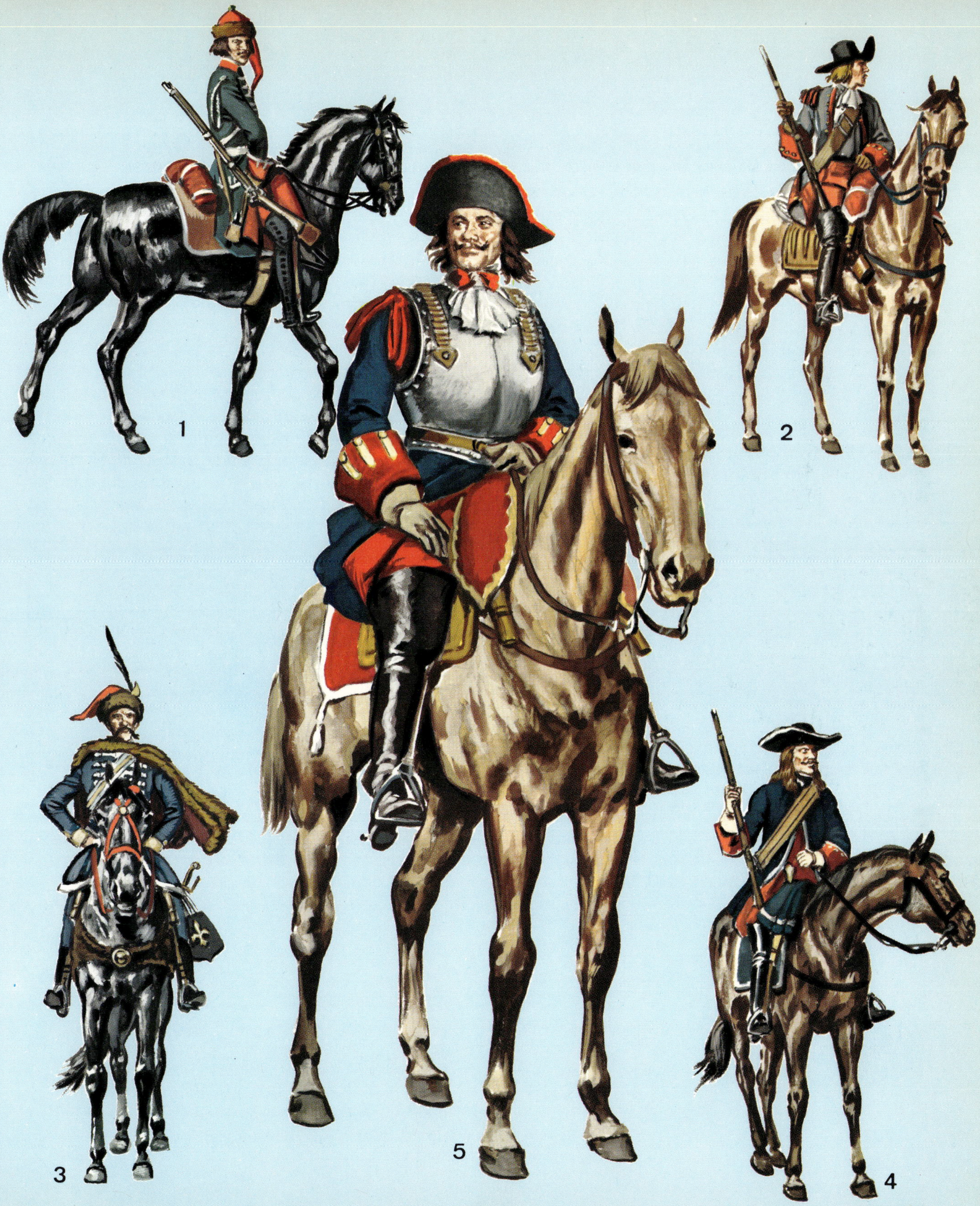
1
2
3
5
4

During the campaigns of Louis XIII, a Neopolitan gentleman, Blaise-Francois de Pagan, further perfected the art of the siege. His treatise on fortifications provided an unknown French officer, Vauban, with the ideas that enabled him to evolve the system to which he later gave his name. Vauban's system was the saving of France between 1709 and 1713 and again under the First Republic in 1793. It was said that "a town fortified by Vauban is an impregnable town". Vauban built thirty-three fortresses and restored more than three hundred others.

A Polish knight, named Pasck, who was present at the siege of a Danish fortress occupied by Swedes under Gustavus Adolphus, has left us in his memoirs a lively account of a 17th Century siege. He writes: "At nightfall, we went in search of axes to break down the gates and collected over five hundred of them. In the morning, we sent a trumpeter to the besieged to call upon them to surrender, but their reply was hardly satisfactory. 'Behave to us' they said, 'as may please your knightly fancy. We were not afraid of you in Poland, you do not frighten us any more here.' Soon the signal for a general attack was given. In my detachment I ordered 'Praise ye the Lord from the heavens, praise him in the heights' (Ps 148) to be sung. Wolski, whose detachment was close to mine, did the same, and God vouchsafed that not one of our soldiers should be killed, while the enemy and Death decimated the other detachments. Each man carried a large truss of straw as a protection against bullets, and, when thrown into the moat, served to form a bridge. Once over, I ordered my men to step out, exhorting them with cries of 'Jesus! Mary!' Others cried 'Hurray, hurray!', but I was confident that Jesus and Mary would protect us better than Sire Hurray. Bullets were falling like hail. More than one soldier cried out in agony, more than one fell to the ground, but we took great cheer because the dead fell with their faces turned towards the enemy, an omen that many soldiers regard as a sure sign of victory. I saw a window surrounded by an iron grille and at once ordered my men to force an entry. As soon as the opening was wide enough to let a man pass, Wolski – devil that he was for being the first anywhere – put his head through, but at that moment a Swede seized him by the hair. Wolski began to yell at the top of his voice. I seized him by the legs. The Swedes were pulling on their side, we on ours, so that our brave companion was in danger of being torn in two! In a low voice, I ordered my men to fire through the window. They fired a few shots and, taken by surprise, the Swedes let go. We climbed in one after the other and, when more than five hundred of us were inside the fortress, I ordered them to open fire and go in with their swords. And, what a fight it was! You

OTHER CAVALRY

1, officer, Belgian dragoons (1690). 2, Hanoverian cavalry (1700). 3, Brandenburg cavalry (1700). 4, trooper, Regiment 'Gens d'Armes' (Germany 1700). 5, Austria-Hungary (1683). 6, Sardinia (1690). 7, dragoon (England, 1672). 8, cornet, 2nd Horse (England, 1685). 9, Bavarian cuirassier (1683).

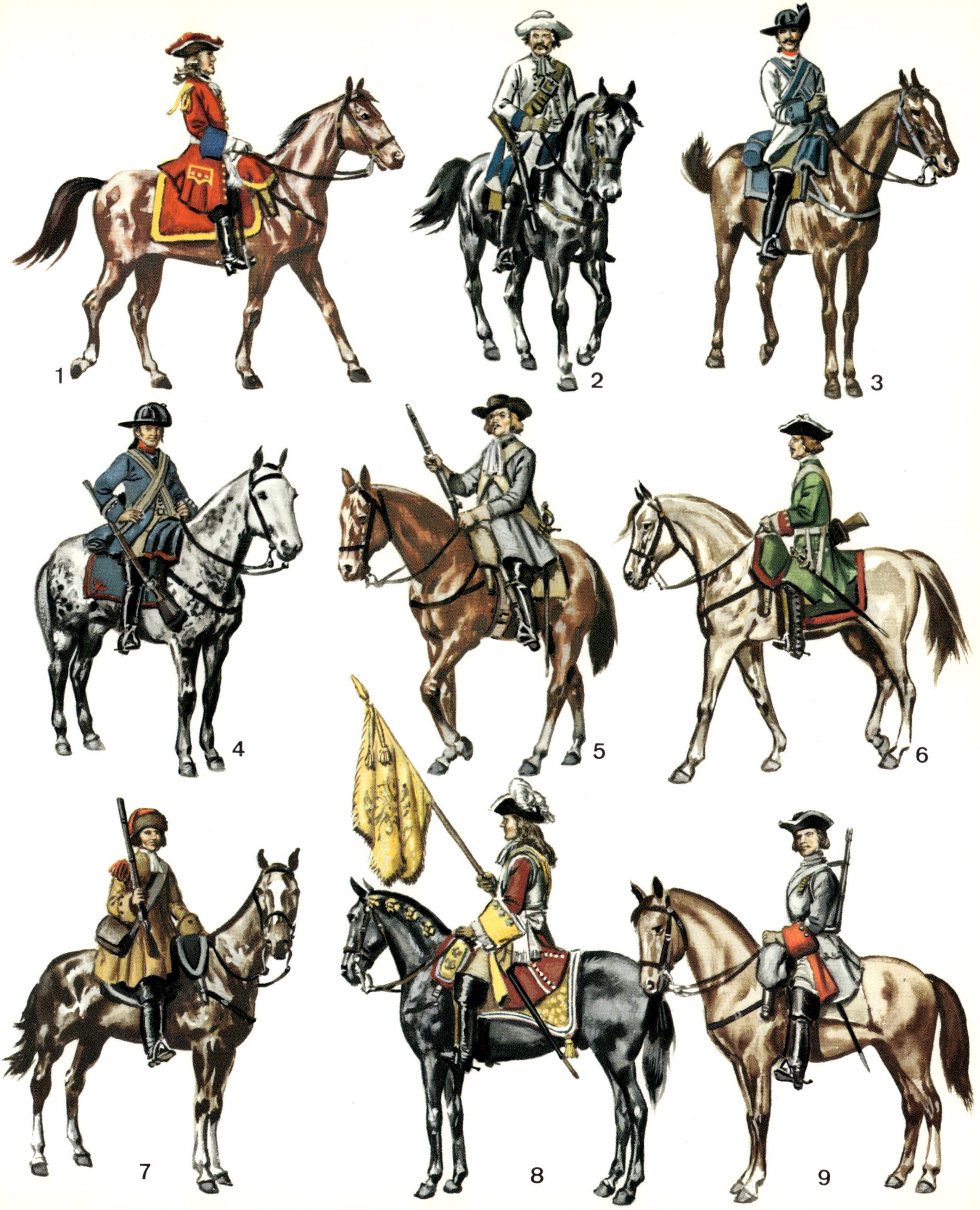
1
2
3
4
5
6
7
8
9

had to be able to see out of the back of your head, for no sooner had you dealt with one man, than another was there about to break your neck."

Later, in his narrative, Pasck gives his views on the siege of Vienna in 1683:

"Vienna, under constant attack, its defences in ruins, mined all around, its guns silenced, was reduced to the last extremity but its garrison had still to be reckoned with. The Commander, General Staremberg, was a brave soldier, powder and provisions were not short – but to what avail was this against these modern methods of assault?... I can assure you that there is not a fortress under the sun capable of standing up to them. It was a different matter when men threw stones and javelins and battered walls with machines. But what can you do when bombs and grape-shots begin to whistle, when mortars vomit up their shot as big as a man's head, when you are peppered with fire that goes straight through everything like a gimlet, armour, clothing and penetrates even to the very bones, when men hurl fire that poisons the air you breathe and the water you drink, and just when you think your feet are firmly planted on the earth, you are in danger – you and the great buildings around you – of being blown sky-high in a cloud of smoke."

Luckily for the unhappy Viennese, John Sobieski was not long coming to the rescue.

1, Prussian grenadier (1698). 2, Prussian musketeer (1680). 3, German grenadier (1690). 4, Austria-Hungary (1720). 5, Germany (1690). 6, Sweden. 7, musketeer, Regiment 'Churfurstin Dorothea zu Brandenburg' (1688). Her initials are shown on the cartridge pouch. 8, English grenadier (1680). 9, English artilleryman (1695). 10, Austrian artilleryman (1671). 11, English grenadier (1689). 12, 13, English foot soldiers (1689).

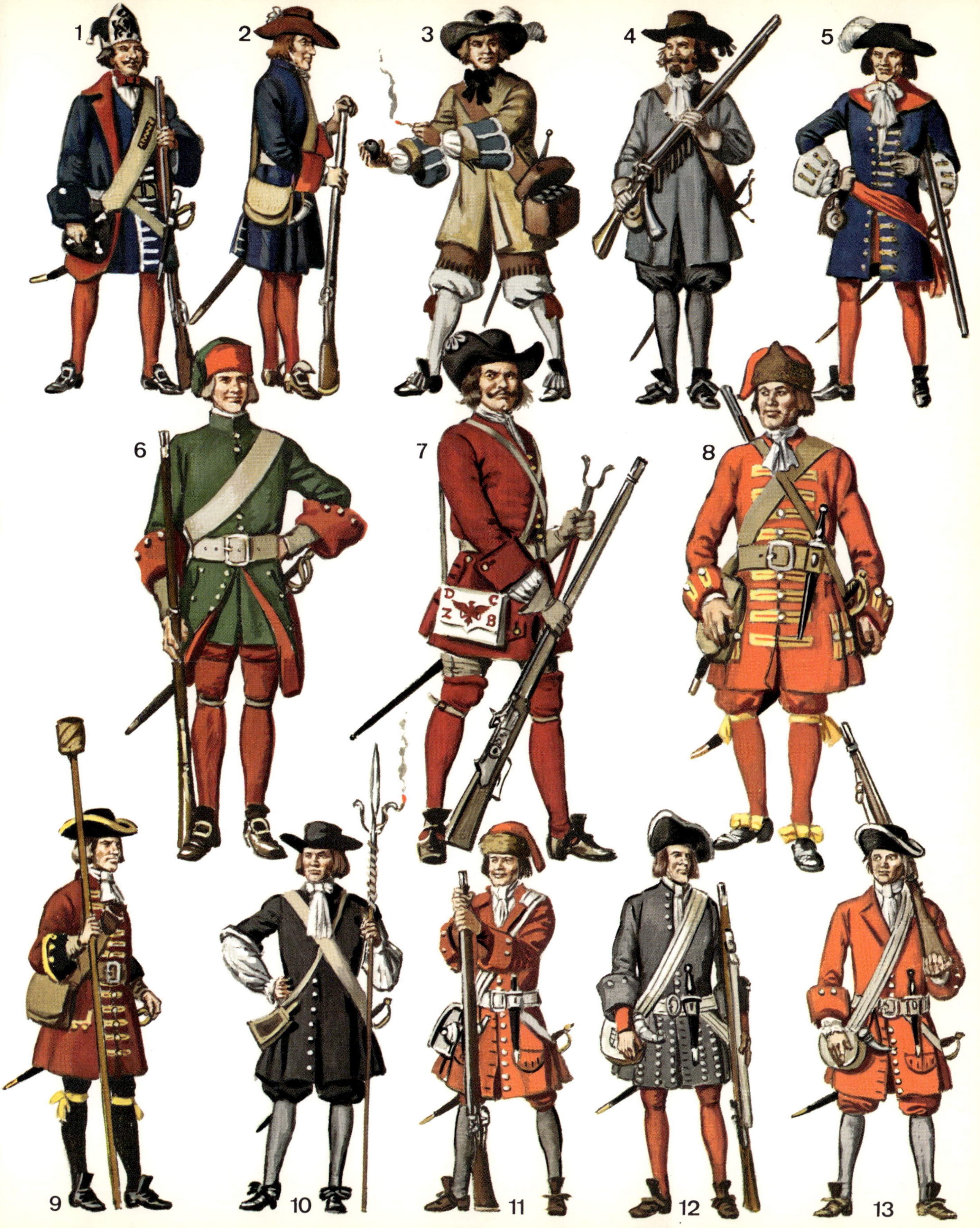
1
2
3
4
5
6
7
8
9
10
11
12
13

The Armies of the First Half of the 18th Century

The lead set by Gustavus Adolphus in distinguishing his regiments by the colour of the uniform was gradually followed by the armies of other nations. From 1680, the various corps were differentiated by the basic colour of the uniform, and the regiments of a corps by the contrasting colours of certain parts, the linings, the collars, and facings of the coats, the waistcoats, and the breeches. Nevertheless, apart from the distinctive colours, uniforms were still the same as civilian dress.

In France, the infantry were usually dressed in white; blue and red was worn by Household Troops and the foreign regiments in the French service. Austria, too, adopted white, while other countries of the Germanic branch of the Holy Empire chose sky-blue (Bavaria), dark-blue (Brandenburg), red and black (Saxony), and so on. Most English regiments were dressed in red.

The old broad-brimmed felt hat gave way to the more elegant and practical tricorne, caps[1] appeared, then the mitre cap[2] of the grenadier. This last type of head-dress was less popular in France than in other countries, where it was adopted by numerous regiments and remained in fashion for a long time, particularly in Prussia.

The artillery were usually dressed in darker colours.

Musicians were distinguished from the rank and file by a profusion of lace on the sleeves right up to the shoulders and on the body of the coat. Kettle-drummers marched at the head of cavalry regiments. In France, the Household Troops were the first to have them. It was customary to allow captured drums to be carried by the Regiments that had taken them, the first to appear in the army of Louis XIV being German. Kettle-drummers were often negroes, as in Villeroy's and the Colonel-General's Regiments. Musicians needed to be especially brave and to be prepared to defend their instruments with their lives. They were often given a mounted escort. A regiment that had distinguished itself in some special way was sometimes awarded silver kettle-drums. The great composers of the age did not think it beneath their dignity to write military marches – Lully composed several pieces with martial rolls on the kettle-drum.

Armies in the field became progressively larger. The French army numbered 400,000 men during the war with Holland, and 440,000 at the time of the League of Augsburg (1691).

Recruiting sergeants resorted to every means to get the recruits the army needed so badly, including trickery or force. They even went so far as locking up their victims to coerce them into signing on.[3] But even these shameful expedients did not bring in the required numbers and provincial militia, formed of men between the ages of 20 and 40, chosen by ballot, were raised. Badly trained and poorly

1 p. 141, *8/11*.   2 p. 143, *8*; p. 149, *2/6/9*.
3 Most often, the generously distributed wine was enough.

INFANTRY AND FOOT ARTILLERY OF LOUIS XV

1, 5, officers. 2, foot soldiers. 3, 4, artillery. 6, ensign, Regiment of the Queen (1757). 7, light infantry. 8, grenadier. 9, alpine infantry. 10, foot guards. 11, plug bayonets. 12, Vauban's fusil. 13, Charleville fusil (1717). 14, Charleville fusil (1746). 15, 16, 17, socket bayonets. 18, miquelet-lock. 19, flint-lock.

143

equipped, the militia were held in contempt by the professional soldiers, in spite of their devoted service in war-time. Louvois had tried to form a pool of future commanders by setting up cadet schools. Under Louis XV, they were reorganized and began to teach military subjects, equitation, and – dancing. The famous equitation school at Saumur dates from this period.

In 1751, the cadet schools became the Ecole Militaire, which, as well as military subjects, taught deportment and etiquette. It is quite true that Madame de Pompadour was behind its creation! "You leave," said Bonneville, "almost as much a child as when you went there."

For the sons of the rich nobility the problem was simple, and the versatility of the age helped: one merely bought a regiment, with the result that there were colonels of eight and ten years old – *Colonels a la bavette* (Colonels in bibs), as they were called. When they were old enough to serve, they made bad officers.

THE CAVALRY

The cavalry was made up mainly of cuirassiers, dragoons and police, who followed the fashions set by the infantry. The hussars were sharply distinguished from the rest of the army by their bizarre equipment. They were introduced at the end of the reign of Louis XIII, and were formed into a single regiment, 500 strong, in 1662. Their colonel was a German, the Baron of Cornesburg. There has been a good deal of argument about the derivation of the word hussar. One theory maintains it comes from the Hungarian *huszard* (the twentieth, from *husz*, twenty), because each village had to provide one fully equipped man for every twenty of its inhabitants; another says it comes from *hus'ar*, which in Hungarian meant twenty sous, the hussar's daily pay.

In French service, they sported a fleur-de-lis in their caps. They were dressed in the Turkish fashion in a tight jacket and baggy trousers, with nothing at all underneath. To protect themselves against the cold they wore a leopard-skin, which they would turn to whichever quarter the wind was coming from. They observed certain strange customs: their officers are said never to have ordered them to charge without first asking their consent. Nothing could make them give up any enemy standard that they had captured because they were in the habit of melting down the gold embroidery on them. The hussars rode small horses and their saddles were of wood with sheep-skin covers. They were armed with pistols, carbine and a 'scimitar' (Turkish sword). Having no pockets, they carried a deerskin bag at their belts, the 'sabretache'.

There were also German hussars such as the Beausabre, and the Polish and Turkish Regiments. Some of the most famous of these regiments were the Rattky, Bercheny, Esterhazy and Chamborand.

CAVALRY OF LOUIS XV
1, Regiment Clermont-Prince (1750). 2, light horseman, Regiment of Fischer (1754). 3, Regiment lately of Turenne. 4, dragoon (1724). 5, 6, dragoon and lancer, Regiment of Marshal Saxe (1762). 7, cuirassier (1730). 8, cavalry carbine and pistol. 9, cavalry waistbelt and cartridge-pouch.

145

One or two items of equipment distinguished the dragoons and musketeers from the rest of the cavalry. As they were liable to have to fight on foot or on horseback, the dragoons wore long gaiters or 'spatterdashes'. They also wore a bonnet, like a nightcap, with a long tassel hanging down over the shoulder;[1] later, this gave way to the Schomberg helmet,[2] worn by the Saxon dragoons. Musketeers still wore the blue surcoat with the silver cross. However, dress regulations were not always obeyed, witness the introduction of the fur cap into the French army.

The Prussian infantry in the time of the 'Serjeant-King' (father of Frederick the Great) included grenadiers who wore a fur-cap that had been designed by the monarch himself. When throwing grenades, the fusil was slung diagonally across the body, but the barrel often caught against the brim of the hat, knocking it off. Frederick William hit upon the idea of substituting for the round hat a pointed bonnet which he ornamented with a brass plate. To give the head-dress a more martial appearance, it was covered with bearskin.

The French were taken with this head-dress and adopted it for the horse grenadiers, and later for the grenadiers of infantry regiments – notwithstanding that the grenade had already become obsolete.

At the same time, the fashion of powdered wigs spread to the army. To stop these leaving grease-marks on the collar of the coat, the men were made to grow pigtails which were just as dirty. Maurice of Saxony (Marshall Saxe) tried to put an end to these absurd practices. He considered that soldiers ought to shave their heads and be allowed to wear little sheepskin wigs, when not on active service. However, he was regarded as an eccentric and the soldiers continued to suffer from the whims of fashion.

WEAPONS

All troops wore buff waistbelts and shoulder-belts. In the certain regiments, these were embellished with silk braid.

In the cavalry, the equipment was yellow, in the infantry white. Foot-soldiers wore the cartridge-pouch on the right and on the left a frog to support the bayonet and the sword. A powder horn for the priming powder and a pouch for the shot hung from the bandolier shoulder belt. Infantry carried muskets; carbines[3] and pistols were only carried by cavalry. All soldiers carried swords, except hussars who had scimitars.

[1] p. 137, *1*; p. 139, *7*; p. 145, *5*.
[2] p. 145, *5*.   [3] A small musket.

OTHER CAVALRY II

1, Flemish musketeer in the Spanish service (1702). 2, Austrian dragoon (1790). 3, Russian dragoon (1765). 4, Prussian hussar (1780). 5, Würtemberg (1787). 6, Prussia (1735). 7, British Horse Grenadier (1750). 8, Prussian hussar (1758).

147

Towards 1740, a similar weapon, though somewhat shorter, was issued to some companies of grenadiers. This was known as the *coupe-chouse* (cabbage cutter). For a long time to come, grenadiers were to be proud of this mark of distinction.

These changes of course came about only gradually, indeed, almost surreptitiously, for politicians fear innovation.

The Comte d'Argenson, the French War Minister, from 1743 to 1757, introduced important reforms made necessary by the state of his army. Barracks were built – in which, however, men slept three to one narrow bed. An army medical service was set up. Henceforward, the responsibility for clothing the army became that of the government (as distinct from that of individual colonels).

In England, the Royal Regiment of Fusiliers was the first to adopt the fusil,[1] which had been developed from the musket by the French. Their duty was to escort the artillery. Devastating explosions were often caused by the sputtering matches of the out-of-date muskets with which the men were at first issued.

The pike as a weapon had by now completely disappeared, though it remained in the form of the spontoon[2] carried by the officers of every nation.

In Russia, the energetic Czar Peter the Great disbanded the mutinous Strelitz[3] and built up a modern army for his country.

TACTICS

The fighting normally happened during the summer and stopped by common consent when the weather deteriorated to allow everyone to take up winter quarters. The armies lived off the countries they occupied, usually at this time Belgium and Holland, which made an ideal battle-ground for the struggle between France and England. John Churchill, Duke of Marlborough, won immortality on the fields of Blenheim, Ramillies, Oudenarde and Malplaquet. The size of the forces involved can be judged from casualties at the battle of Blenheim: 23,000 killed or wounded.

Attacks on fortified towns were carried out in much the same way as before, but with an increased use of mines by both sides. At the siege of Tournai in 1709, for example, on August 16th, a single mine blew up 400 men. In general, the military commanders of the first half of the century were fairly evenly matched, but the whole of Europe was soon to have to reckon with a formidable military power: the Prussia of Frederick II the Great.

1 p. 143, *13–14.* 2 p. 135, *4–5*; p. 143, *1/5.* 3 p. 149, *1.*

1, Russia (1780). 2, Brandenburg (1700). 3, Scots Highlander (1745): the spike on the shield was detachable. 4, 5, grenadiers, Walloon Guards, in the Spanish service (1761 and 1745). 6, British grenadier in marching order (1751). 7, British marine (1742). 8, British light infantry (1758). 9, 'Giant Grenadier', Frederick William of Prussia, the Serjeant-King (1730). 10, Scottish pistol. 11, English pistol (1740). 12, English pistol (1760). 13, French pistol (1770).

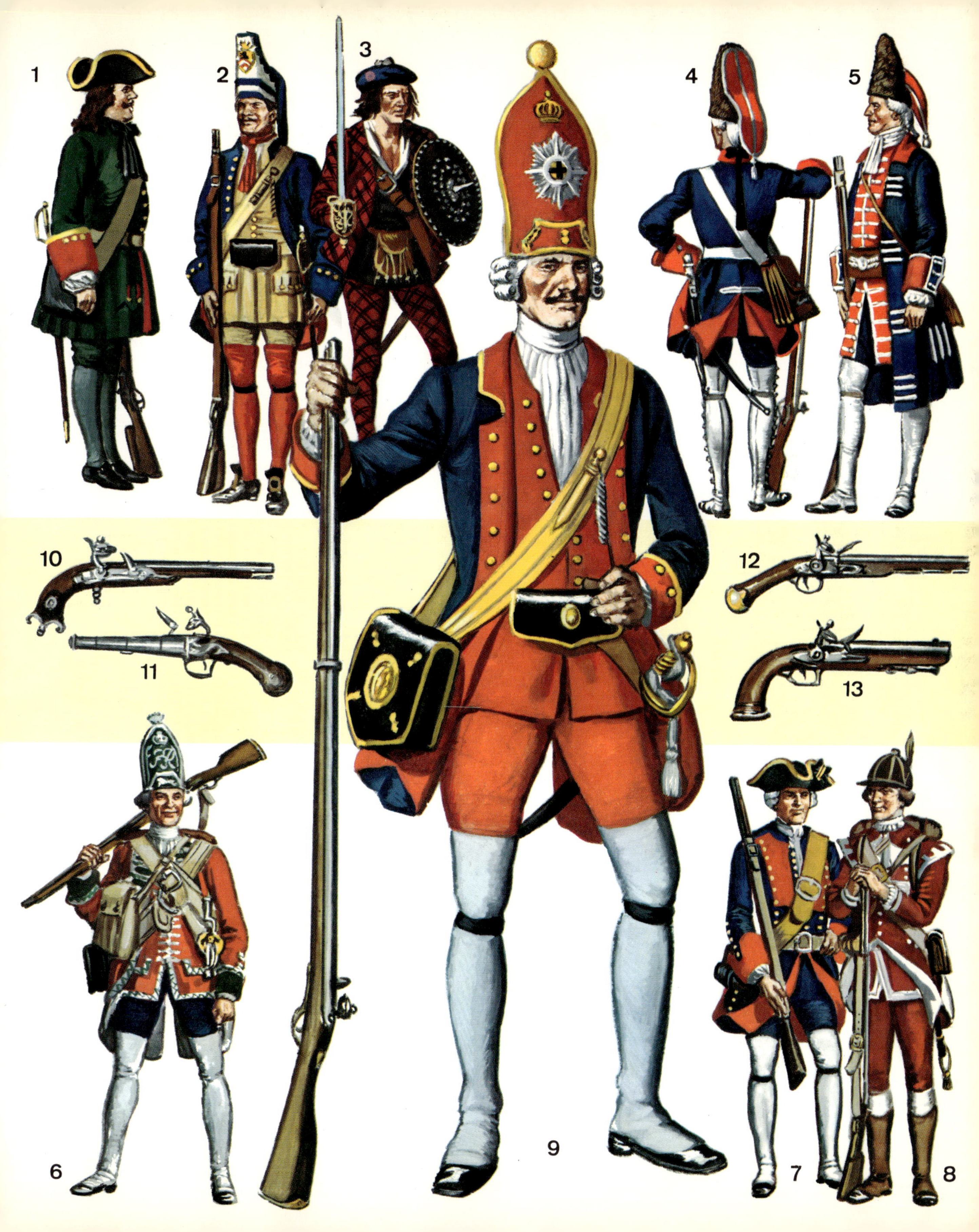
1
2
3
4
5
6
7
8
9
10
11
12
13

Index

Acontistes 42
Adb-er-Rahman 86
Aeneas 34
Aeytius 82
Agathias 84
Agincourt 106
Alauda legion 56
Alexander the Great 44, 48, 72
Allobroges 74
America 90
Amphi theatre 70
Angles 86
Antioch 100
Arabs 86
Argenson, Comte d' 148
Armenia 16
Armour 12, 14, 18, 20, 24, 32, 36, 38, 58, 74, 88, 94, 102, 108, 110, 120, 124
Armorial bearings 80
Arquebus 114, 116, 122, 124, 126
Arrow 28, 92, 94
Arthur, King 86
Artillery 118, 136
Artillery, Loading of 132
Artois, Robert d' 106
Ashurnasirpal 16
Ass 20, 22
Assurbanipal 16, 22
Assyria 10, 16
Attic helmet 38
Attila 82

Augustus, Emperor 54, 62
Aurelius 84
Auxiliaries 56, 62
Axe 14, 76, 80, 84, 92

Babylon 22, 26
Ballista 66
Bannockburn 108
Basinet 96
Battering-ram 20, 66, 100
Bayonet 128
Belshazzar 26
Berbers 98
Belgae 76
Bertrand du Guesclin 108, 110
Black Prince 112
Bladder 18
Blenheim 148
Boat 18
Boeotian helmet 42
Bohemund of Antioch 100
Bombs 122
Bonneville 144
Bossuet 136
Bow and arrows 12, 18, 24, 28, 34, 82, 88, 90, 98, 108
Breech 112
Brennus 72
Brittany 86
Bronze 30

Cabasset 120

Calego 60
Calibre 130
Cambyses 28
Camel 24, 26
Camillus 54, 58
Cannon 112
Capitulaires 88
Caracole 120
Carbine 146
Carrier pigeon 90
Cartridge 130
Cataphractus 64
Catapult 66
Cavalry 18, 24, 42, 44, 54, 64, 86, 90, 108, 116, 122
Chaldea 16
Chamfron 102, 122
Chandos, John 108, 110
Chariot 10, 16, 18, 20, 24, 70, 76, 78
Charlemagne 86, 88, 90
Charles V of Germany 116
Charles VIII 120
Charles Martel 86, 98
Charles the Simple 92
Cicero 70
Clipeus 58
Clothyard 96
Cohort 56
Colonel-General's Regiment 142
Commentaries 78

Constantinople 90, 98
Corinthian Bronze 30
Corinthian helmet 36, 38
Coupe chouse 148
Crepides 40
Croesus 24, 26
Cromwell 124, 126
Crossbow 96, 98, 108, 112
Crusade 98, 100
Cuirass 122
Cuirassers 122, 126, 144
Culverin 114
Cutlass 80, 84
Cyrus 24

Dagger 14, 24, 28, 34, 76, 124
Damascus 100
Darius I 28, 44
Diomedes 36
Dorian helmet 38
Dragoons 128, 144
Duke d'Enghien 134, 136
Duke of Lancaster 110
Duke of Marlborough 148

Eagle 56
Ecole Militaire 144
Edward the Confessor 92
Edward II 108
Edward III 108, 112
Egypt 10
El Cid 98

Elephant 44, 66
Engineers 20
Errard, Jean 136
Esarhaddon 16
Etruscans 52
Euphrates 10, 16, 26
Excalibur 86

Firearms 112
Flintlock 128
Flute 48
Fort 78, 80, 92, 100, 136
Francis I 120, 122
Frederick I of Prussia 146
Frederick II of Prussia 148
Froissart, Jean 102, 108
Fuse 126
Fusil musket 130
Fusiliers 130, 148
Fyrd 92

Gaul 52, 56, 64, 72, 80
Gibraltar 90
Gerrhe 24
Godfrey de Bouillon 98
Goedenag 102
Greaves 32, 36, 60
Greece 12, 28, 72
Gregory of Tours 84
Grenade 130
Grenadier 126, 130, 142, 146, 148
Guiart 102

Gustavus Adolphus 124, 130, 132, 138, 142
Gypoun 96

Hackbut 114
Hadrian 66
Hannibal 62, 74
Harold 92
Hastings 92
Hastatii 54
Hauberk 96, 100
Helmet 10, 18, 20, 32, 36, 38, 58, 74, 80, 86, 90, 94, 102, 110, 120, 122
Henry II of France 118, 120
Henry IV of France 126
Hipposandals 42, 64
Hittites 10
Homer 30, 32
Hoplite 36, 44
Hoqueton 90
Horus 10
House-carl 92
Hun 80, 82
Hungary 82
Hussars 144
Hyskos 10

Iberian sword 62
Iliad 30, 32
Immortals 28
Infidel 98

152

Iran 24
Iron 30
Ishtar 16

Javelin 12, 18, 20, 34, 42, 54, 62, 74, 80, 82, 84, 90
Jerusalem 98, 100
John, King 104
Joinville, Jean, Sire de 90
Judea 16
Julius Caesar 56, 60, 70, 78

Kettledrums 142
Knallbuchsen 114
Kopersh 10

Laconian way 48
Lance 94, 116, 126
Lansquenets 120
Lateran Council 98
League of Augsburg 142
Legions 54
Lightning Legion 60
Lietard of Tournai 100
Linstock 118
Lion-ts'ong 80
Livy 54
Louis III 90
Louis XII 122
Louis XIII 134, 138, 144
Louis XIV 118, 120, 142
Louis XV 144

Louvois 124, 144
Lully, Jean-Baptiste 142
Luna 96
Lydia 12, 24

Mace 24, 76, 102, 116
Macedonian way 48
Mackay, General Donald 130
Mangonel 112
Maniple 56
Manse 88
Mantlet 66
Marathon 40
Marius 56, 58, 62
Marshal Saxe 146
Massacres 20, 84
Matchlock 114, 118
Maximilian armour 112
Measuring staff 124
Media 24
de Mello, Don Francisco 134
Mercenaries 12, 62, 88, 120, 122
Merovingians 86
Mesopotamia 16
Militia 144
Mine 148
Misericord 124
Mongol 80
Monluc 116
Montaigne 78
Montecuculli, General 130
Montesquieu, Charles 62

Morion 120, 122
Mummius 30
Musicians 142
Musket 114, 118

Nabonidus 24
Net 70, 82
New Model Army 124
Normans 92

Odyssey 30
Ogre 82
Onager 66
Otho IV of Germany 104

de Pagan, Blaise-Francois 138
Parazonium 34, 40
Paris of Troy 34
Parma 58
Parsargadea 24
Pasck 138, 140
Paulus Emilius 48
Peloponnesian war 42
Pelta 40
Peltastes 42
Perrault, Charles 82
Persia 24
Peter the Great 148
Phalanx 40, 44
Philippe II Auguste 98, 104
Philippe VI 108
Phrygia 26

Pike   12, 102, 126, 148
Pikeman   122
Pilum   56, 62, 64
Pistol   120, 122
Polybius   40, 46, 50, 60
Pompadour, Madame de   144
Pompeii   70
Procopius   28, 84
Prussia   142, 148
Psiletes   42
Punic War, Second   64
de Puysegur   128

Quillon   102

Ramesis II   10
Ramesis III   10
Recruiting   142, 144
Reiter   120
Retiary   70
Richard I   98
Richelieu, Cardinal   136
Robert Bruce   108
Rome   52, 72
Rope   70
Russia   28, 148

Sabre   90
Sabretache   144
Sackbut   102
Sagum   72
Saint-Pol, Comte de   104, 106

Saladins   100
Samnite   70
Saps   20
Sardis   24, 26
Sargon   16
Sarissa   40, 46
Sarmatians   64, 84
Sash   126
Saumur   144
Saxons   86
Scaling ladder   20
Schomberg helmet   146
Scimitar   146
Scorpion   66
Scramsax   80, 84
Scutum   60
Scythe   24, 102
Scythian   28
Sennacherib   16
Serjeant-King   146
Servius Tullius   54, 58, 64
Shield   12, 14, 18, 24, 32, 36, 38, 58, 60, 74, 80, 84, 88
Sidonius Appolinarius   84
Siege of Vienna   140
Siege-tower   20
Sirot   134
Sling   14, 34, 76
Sobieski, John   140
Spartha   62, 80
Spear   12, 24, 28, 36, 84, 88
Sphendonetes   42

Splatterdashes   146
Stavemberg, General   140
Steel   30
Strelitz   148
Strozzi, Admiral   116
Sudan   12
Suez   10
Sword   14, 18, 40, 62, 74, 80, 82, 84, 88, 94, 116
Sylla   70
Syria   16

Tarik   90
Tercios   136
Terraces   26
Tetraphalanx   44
Teutates   78
Thebes   16
Thotmosis   10
Thracian   70
Tiara   24
Tigalathpileser I   16
Timolos   24
Tollenon   66
Tortoise   66
Tower of Babel   16
Toxotes   42
Trajan   58
Trebuchet   112
Tricorne   142
Tripolitania   12

Trojan War 30
Trumpet 48
Turks 98, 100

Uniforms 124, 130, 142

Vauban 130, 138
Velites 54
Villeroy's Regiment 142
Visor 32, 70, 96, 102

Walhousen 128
Wheel-lock 120
Wig 10, 18, 146
William I 92

Xenophon 42

Yue-tche 80